SH!T YOGIS SHOULDN'T SAY

DR. TRACEY L. ULSHAFER

Copyright © 2025 Dr. Tracey L. Ulshafer

www.OneYogaCenter.net
www.TraceyUlshafer.com

All rights reserved.

No unauthorized reproduction of any parts of this book's contents or cover for any reason without the expressed consent of Rev. Dr. Tracey L. Ulshafer.

ISBN: 979-8-9860235-6-4

DEDICATION

This book is dedicated to my grandmothers, Rachel and Genevieve, who have both transitioned.

Rachel loved to curse, especially when watching the Philadelphia Phillies. Genevieve, who we affectionately called Nanny, rarely had a bad word to say until she was in her 90s, when she finally began to cut loose. She only cursed in Italian. And that was the only Italian I ever heard her speak.

Neither of my grandmothers was a yogi. But I'd like to think they'd both get a kick out of this book. Either that or they'd be completely appalled. Oh well. Fuck it. Here we go...

TABLE OF CONTENTS

Dedication	3
Table of Contents	4
Prologue	5
Fuck	13
I Hate That Pose	25
Wanna Hit Mickey D's?	36
Does My Ass Look Fat In These Lululemons?	48
Namaste	59
My Third Eye Is Blocked	71
That's Never Going To Happen, I'm Being Realistic	82
I Am My Own Guru	94
Epilogue	106
Glossary	108
Other Books By Tracey	121
"The Vault" Yoga	122
About the Author	123

PROLOGUE

Welcome to *Sh!t Yogi's Shouldn't Say*. If you are reading this book, it is most likely for one of two reasons: First, it was a catchy title that got your attention, and you are an impulse buyer. Thank you! Secondly, you practice *yoga* but do not walk around with a stick up your ass about it. Surely, in our world, you know at least one person who attests to being a *yogi/yogini*, holding everyone else accountable for their actions, yet hides behind their hypocrisy. I've always tried to be as transparent as possible about any of my sanctimonious bullshit as they were brought to my awareness. Yes, I'm human like all of you. Even *yogis* make mistakes and continue learning lessons throughout their lives. Why else are we here? Be real. Be messy. But always be loving and true.

Let me start by saying that nobody should tell anyone else what he or she should or should not say. I'm a big fan of free speech. I received an accommodation in Journalism from my college and was well on my way to being a journalist when Dan Rather told me and a room full of inspiring college newspaper junkies to quit while we were ahead. Seriously, he did. It was probably the worst motivational speech I've ever heard. He just told us all to find another career choice. Anyway, let's hear it for the First Amendment! All hail, James Madison!

Not only can you say whatever you want, but those words have nothing to do with you being considered a practitioner of *yoga*. There are no *yoga* police, although some may proclaim that they are. Most *yoga* teachers acknowledge that there are certain guidelines as to what constitutes being a *yogi*. I'll dive into those concepts under a modern lens while still attempting to honor this thousands-year-old self-development practice that I and so many others have come to realize as a life-saving methodology. And when I say life-saving, I do mean that literally. As any modern-day *yogi* attests, having *yoga* in my life may, like the popular t-shirt says, "keep me from killing people."

I'm also not here to tell you what to think, how to talk, or how to act. But since I've been around the block with this *yoga* practice for a bit, I am simply conveying messages I've come to understand in my sarcastic, blunt, New Jerseyan way. So, at least give me the benefit of reading the book in its entirety before you pick it apart and share only the pieces that you may find offensive — which I am confident there may be at least one. How do we "stretch" and grow if we aren't challenged by someone or something? Finding yourself offended is an opportunity to dig into your judgments, traumas, and deep-held karmic residues for healing. I share what I share with love. And love isn't always an easy path. But it's a true one.

Before I launch too deeply into the content, I hear some of you sniffing around about my credentials. What makes me someone who knows anything about *yoga* or being a *yogi*? This is an honest question that I've asked myself a thousand times. I believe a true follower of any spiritual path ponders these things. I sincerely still consider it. I flip back and forth between feeling completely inadequate and incompetent and being on the level of the grand *yogi*-master Lord *Shiva* himself. I'm confident that the truth is that I'm locked solidly somewhere in the middle. But for those who wish to know more about me, here's the scoop:

Somewhere in the 1990s, I began practicing *yoga*. I was in my twenties then and was suffering from ongoing pain in my back due to a compression fracture that I'd gotten in a car accident at 15 years old. There are moments in your life that happen in a flash but change the course of your life in monumental ways. Thus was an April evening in 1985, when my boyfriend misjudged a turn, hit a ditch, and flipped his 1972 Mustang upside down — with me in the passenger seat wearing just a lap belt. Years later, I would look at my spine on an X-ray and discover a chip in my first Lumbar vertebra from the accident. This weak link in my chain, coupled with the fact that I was quite lazy, caused instability where my back "gave out" at the first sign of anything strenuous. It was getting a little annoying and starting to cramp my lifestyle. So, my friend suggested that I try *yoga* to see if it would help me. She was probably tired of hearing me bitch about my back, too.

I hated *yoga* at first. I didn't think it was relaxing. I couldn't stop my wandering mind. The poses were difficult. And I sincerely hated final relaxation. But after several weeks, I realized that I was no longer reaching for Advil multiple times a day. In fact, I hadn't had one in, well, I'd lost track of when. It was with vigor and confidence that I dove into a regular *yoga* practice, and it completely changed my life.

A few years later, I quit my corporate job with benefits and "stability" (much to the dismay of my family) after graduating from a holistic massage school and a 500-hour *yoga* teacher training program. It was the turn of the century. Wow, that makes me sound so old. Anyway, it was 2000. While most of the world was euphoric over surviving Y2K (look it up), I nonchalantly began my career in holistic healing practices. I opened my wellness center, started a *yoga* school, and kept expanding my studios and offerings. I tallied that between my regular *yoga* classes, workshops, and teacher trainings, I'd racked up just under 22,000 teaching hours in the practice of *yoga* in my first 22 years.

In that time, I trained and practiced with well-known *yogi* teachers such as Shiva Rea, Baron Baptiste, Sri Dharma Mittra, Sean Corn, and others. I went to Yoga Journal conventions and spent time at the Kripalu Center for Yoga & Health in Massachusetts taking various workshops and staying in the former *Ashram* for needed R&R. I eventually even made it to *yoga's* Motherland, India, and spent a little time at the *Sivananda Ashram* in Kerala, where I realized quite early on that I hated it. I wanted to love it. A good *yogi* would have loved it, right?

Let's just say that this *ashram* living was not for me. First of all, I require lots of sleep, and the strenuous schedule hampered that. Secondly, I am not an early riser — ask anyone who knows me. Tracey before 11 am is like a rabid animal. Stay away. I will say, the Chai we received mid-morning tamed the beast within a tad. There is truly nothing like the Chai in India. And that brings me to the third thing: it was dirty. I don't do well with dirty. I'll spare you the details. I know we don't know each other that well, but I'm asking you to trust me. So, after a few days of sweating and stinking, eating with my hands while trying to remember which hand was for wiping and which one was for eating, not getting enough sleep, and being unable to find a comfortable position on the hard meditation room floor, I revolted. And I took some students with me.

I spent the last night at the *Sivananda Ashram* hiding out in my room with three of my students, watching the movie *Superbad* on my iPhone. For your edification, I also had *The 40-Year-Old Virgin* and *Step Brothers* locked and loaded on said iPhone. That should tell you everything you need to know about my sense of humor. And before you think that it discolors my credit to being a true *yogi*, I'll tell you that we were leaving for Thailand the next day, and Thailand is a Buddhist culture, and Buddhists are austere *yogis* themselves. I'm a big fan of the Buddha and his "Middle Path." So, try a little meditation; use a little cursing. Do a little *pranayama*; watch a little bit of a stupid movie. You get my point.

Although I am making a lot of jokes, I never took teaching *yoga* lightly. Whenever I took another workshop, training, or class with a new teacher, I felt myself being initiated into the sacred healing art more deeply. Teaching *yoga* became a ritual in channeling the *yoga* teachers that came before me. I opened myself up and allowed the ancient teachings to move through me. I rarely remembered what I taught students in any particular class, but I often heard it was pretty cool. I figure at this point I've forgotten more about *yoga* than most people today dare to learn. So if you're still wondering what gives me the right to share my thoughts on *yoga* or being a *yogi*, too bad. This is my book, and you bought it.

In my 22 years of owning a *yoga* studio, I realized that there are many judgments regarding *yoga* and being a *yogi* — especially within the *yoga* community. Ironic, isn't it, since most in this community spout the phrase "love and light?" The belief systems, standards, and sometimes downright conceit of some in the industry have even tainted much of the teachings and practices, overlaying them with unusable dogma and misinterpretations. Yup, I said it.

Having spent a huge portion of my career in the field, I closed my beloved *yoga* studio with lots of pent-up agitation about many such things. This book is my cathartic release of all the time and energy I spent holding myself to some ridiculously unattainable high standard as the owner and founder of a spiritual center. For years, I considered starting a support group for *yoga* studio owners, for surely there are certain things that only we will understand. Alas, it never came to be, but perhaps we can pen a second book, including cooperation from some of you (let's circle back after we see how this one goes).

So, I've acquired a little knowledge about this ancient *yoga* practice. While I would never consider myself a *guru* (see Chapter 8) or even a "master teacher" (that one really tickles me), I believe that I can put things into perspective for the common folk with whom I am very much aligned.

If you're easily offended, boy, did you pick up the wrong book! And now you have a very important decision to make. Do you proceed with my very honest caution? Or do you take a pass and give the book to your crazy favorite aunt? Take a moment to think about it. I'll throw in a little fucking cursing for you so that you can consider this significant question one more moment. Shit's about to get real. Can you handle that? Or are your Lululemons riding up to show off your *yoga* ass purposely? Too much? There's your answer.

Hey, is this a good time to bring up those other types of leggings sewn to gather into the ass-crack? Why? They can't be comfortable. Am I showing signs of my age, or is there a need for those in the market? Perhaps I am not the one to talk about it. I was never a *yoga* fashionista. Most of my *yoga* attire came from T.J. Maxx, and I've rarely spent more than $40 on any single pair of *yoga* pants. A pair of pants? Why do we say that? Isn't one just a pant? Be prepared to go down these and other chaotic rabbit holes with me along this journey.

Now that we've broken you in a bit, I must admit that one of my major slogans is: "Everything is Energy." I didn't make that up; Einstein did. But it is a truth that resonates deeply with me. Whenever I ponder the reasons or realities for anything, I go to the energy behind it. When I curse, I realize there is an energy here that may not be airy, sugary, and of the loving kind. I'm fine with that. There's a light and a dark that exists in everything. To ignore the dark or shadow is to deny the half that compliments and thereby creates the whole, unifying oneness.

For me, it's all about intention. And, as I already said, what I convey when I write is meant for the Highest Good of all and comes from my heart. My heart, just like yours, has been broken and holds deep grief and longing. It's also pure love and expands to encompass a cosmic universality of compassion for all that is. Besides, I'm a Gemini, so I've learned to embody the chaos that springs from the duality within while others search to understand me. But the only thing to know is that it's all real and part of the whole.

Okay, if you are still with me and you're ready to have some fun and talk a little *yoga*, let's fucking do this. For those who have passed, thank you for your time. You will not be missed so much, but we will still light a candle for you and honor your brief presence with us. Not really, but at least know that no matter what you do or what I say, Jesus loves us all. And in his ministry of love, he had a particular affection for the degenerates of society. So, for those hanging in with me, know you are in good company. Even Jackasses can be *yogis*. I'm sure I read that in a *Sutra* somewhere, right next to the ancient Lord Vader Breath. You hear it now, don't you? The famous Lord Vader Breath? You're welcome.

So, remember to smile and laugh a lot. Life was meant to be joyful, and if we are weighted down by the heaviness that life can bring, how will we ever learn to levitate? That's why I practice, anyway. Well, that and the mind-reading thing. And the invisibility! *Ashtanga Yoga* founder, Sri Pattabhi Jois said, "Practice and all is coming." I truly believe it. You're missing out if you are in it solely for the *yoga* butt.

Love and Infinite Blessings on this crazy journey of life.

~ Dr. T

CHAPTER 1

FUCK

*"Don't fuck with me fellas.
This ain't my first time at the rodeo."
~ Joan Crawford*

That's right. Let's get right into it, shall we? New Jerseyans (no, we are not all mafia, although we may know of someone who is or was) are known for their direct communication methods, as was pointed out to me by a publishing industry critic several years ago. I thank her for this acknowledgment and have come to accept it as a gift and a blessing. As for the title of this chapter, try to convince me that when you first read this book's title, it wasn't the first word that came to your mind. I know. You can't.

I wish to propose the question, what is your relationship to the word fuck? Take a good moment to reflect. If you are of my generation (Generation X) then fuck is a word solidly sitting in your everyday vernacular. However, if you are, say, a "Baby Boomer," you may have mixed emotions about the word, or, in the case of my mother, loathe it entirely. Sorry, Mom. You can skip to Chapter 2.

Growing up, fuck was not a word that was allowed in our house. My mother made it quite clear how she felt about the word, which she graciously referred to as "The F-word," so I never even dared try it. I did not, in fact, use it even with friends. The word was off-limits to me, and I stayed committed to Mom's feelings on it until somewhere in my college years when the true essence of the word finally landed for me. And since I was commonly referred to by my friends as a "goody-goody," it felt cool to finally be a little naughty when mom was not around. I soon began to integrate fuck into my vocabulary, where it has found its daily home.

When George Carlin famously gave his comedic dialogue about the seven dirty words you cannot say on television, fuck was right up there. And most people understand it to be one of the dirtiest words in the world. Do a quick internet search for uses of fuck, and you will find a litany of blogs and articles, all well-written by many others who came way before me, and who understand the English language a whole lot better than I (me?) as well. However, for the sake of this book, let's break this delicious word down just a bit.

Fuck is quite a versatile little fucker. It can be used as a verb, as in the original dictionary meaning of having sex with someone. But it can also be a noun (fucker; as in the guy who squeezed his *yoga* mat next to you after you had deliberately created a very wide expanse around your mat), an adverb (It's fucking hot as hell in here; as heard from any regular *yogi* entering a hot *yoga* studio for the first time), an adjective (Is she fucking kidding me?; disparaging mental words for the *yoga* teacher about a minute into holding *Utkatasana*, the Sanskrit word for Chair pose — we will talk about the poses in another chapter, hang in there), and an interjection (Fuck!; upon falling on your face whilst attempting *Bakasana* or Crow, an arm balance posture). You can easily see how the use of the word fuck appropriately slides into anyone practicing *yoga's* vocabulary.

Another usage for wishing to honor a person's appropriate pronouns but either get a little confused about it or forget, "Fucker" works rather nicely. Now, before you get offended, please understand that I honestly would call anyone fucker. And, anyway, being offended is your shit. Not mine.

Combining the F-word as a composite, you find a slew of fun options to up the ante, such as:
- Motherfucker - the beautiful pony-tailed *yogi* who has sex with your mother while on retreat in Costa Rica
- Fuck off - a phrase appropriate for those who have an aversion to the scent of lavender and find the teacher at the *yoga shala* rubbing it on their temples during *savasana* (this is the famous Corpse pose used in final relaxation)
- Fuckinator - the big dude from the gym who dropped into your *yoga* class to check out all the cute *yoga* gals and promptly reported that he'll be back
- Etc. and there are lots of etceteras. You can be super creative with these composites to work for just about anyone in any situation. Unleash your 2nd chakra! (We'll tackle the chakras later, too)

In our ever-increasing digital age, where we need to constantly do more in less time, using an acronym instead of typing all of the words out can save you valuable seconds a day.

Example: You arrive at *yoga* class after a hurried day, change in the studio bathroom, and realize that you have a large hole at the inseam of your Lulus — and you're going commando today. You text your *yoga* buddy "OMFG" with a snapshot of the hole (*before* you put the pants on, you dirty bird. Geez! Do you think she would text a freaking picture of the gaping hole in her pants while wearing them? Well, maybe she would, especially if she was from Jersey).

OK, let's put the flipping breaks on a second. Is this a little too much for some of you? I did warn you. Even my husband, the King of potty-mouths just said, 'That's a lot of fucks." I rewrote much of this chapter already to tame it a bit down for the wussies. For those struggling, there's a fabulous YouTube video with Sadhguru on the meaning of, as he puts it, this "magical" word. This popular man has about 8.3 million Instagram followers. So, if an Indian Holy Man can not just say but embrace fuck, maybe it's not that offensive.

Whether you find the word fuck offensive and vulgar or not, we all agree it does elicit a strong reaction from most people when spoken, which is most likely why my generation has embraced it — we're known for being direct. Combine that with the Jersey thing, and boom! We like words that pack a powerful punch. But the question of the day is: would or could or should a *yogi* say fuck?

To properly answer this question, it becomes significant to first understand just who or what a *yogi* is.

On the surface, a *yogi* is anyone who practices *yoga*. Great, now we have to understand what *yoga* is. This topic has produced thousands of books already. So I'm just going to talk about what I have come to understand as *yoga*, from my decades of practicing and teaching it, from the culminated knowledge of the hundred books on it that I've read, and the thousands of hours of it I have taught to others. And if you still wish to take issue with any of what I will share, please feel free to email me at idonotgiveafuk.org (.com was already in use, just kidding, I don't even know).

As I have come to humbly understand, there are many forms of what we know as the practice of yoga, but they all culminate in the intention to unify all the parts of the being to realize the True Self, thus achieving a state of what most people simply call "bliss."

There are five types of *yoga*: *Bhakti*, a devotional style where chanting and prayer are performed to become one with God. *Karma* is an action-based *yoga* whereby the *yogi* strives to master the art of service to others without the need for reciprocity. *Jnana*, the style of *yoga* called "the *yoga* of knowledge," requires the *yogi* to learn and study scriptures constantly. *Hatha* is the most commonly practiced style that uses postures, breathing, meditation, and other techniques to purify the person's body and mind. Finally, *Raja*, considered "The Royal *Yoga*," utilizes many points of all of the other aforementioned styles to prepare the practitioner for ultimate enlightenment.

Most people today practice a form of *Hatha yoga*. *Kundalini* is a type of *Hatha yoga*. *Vinyasa*, *Ashtanga*, Hot *Yoga* (formerly known as *Bikram*), *Iyengar*, Restorative, *Sivananda*, Pre-Natal, Partner, Happy Morning Flow, I Don't Sleep Midnight Burn, and Leave the Goats Alone *Yin* are all types of *Hatha yoga*.

The concept behind all *Hatha yoga*, again, is to purify the mind and body so that it can withstand the higher frequency band that comes with sustained meditative states, thus alleviating the bondage of human suffering and ultimately allowing the being to achieve that *nirvana*-like state while embodied. Or, of course, to achieve a firm buttock and cut arms that you can spotlight while performing a daredevil balancing act on a cliffside for a filtered Instagram post linking to your *yoga* blog — #iamtoocoolforschool.

So now we understand what the practice of *yoga* is. Therefore, anyone, particularly but not limited to the male persuasion, who performs these practices can be called a *yogi*.

The practice of *yoga* originated on the Indian subcontinent thousands of years ago. I will pull back the history on this in a later chapter if you have the patience to wait for it. I know history was spellbinding stuff in high school, but it's even funner now! (If that's not a real word, my editor will cut it out. Or not. Maybe I leave it because I'm a rebel like that). The reason we cannot get a firm date on *yoga* is that the practice was originally an oral tradition, passed down from teacher to disciple. The potential is that *yoga* is much older than we think, but for our purposes in this chapter, it doesn't fucking matter.

My point, and I do have one, is to identify what type of practice *yoga* is so that we can ascertain any universal teachings that may assist us in grappling with the use of the all-mighty vulgar word fuck. If we were to leave it at the physical level, we would understand it as all that we can do for the body, and then those who practice Booty *Yoga* would say, "A-ha! I knew it!" But those who sat down to write about spiritual practices such as *yoga* specifically outlined a layering system within the human person known as the *Koshas*.

The *koshas* consist of the body sheath (*annamayakosha*), vital energy sheath (*pranamaya kosha*), mental (*manomaya kosha*), wisdom body (*vijnanamaya kosha*), and, finally, the bliss body (*anandamayakosha*). I purposely wrote them like that to fuck with those who claim to have OCD. For those who do have OCD, I hear *yoga* helps. Again, my point is that the body is just the outermost, densest layer of our being. It is not the totality of us, and, as we will soon discover, it is certainly not the only part that *yoga* works with.

When we understand *yoga* as the realization of who or what we truly are and eventually come to that bliss body, we begin to tip the scales into the profound levels in which we can classify *yoga*. For it is spirituality, it is science, it is physical, it is energy, it is a natural state of being, and it is a cultivated one, too. And with so many moving parts, it is no surprise that man needed to codify and put words to it, lending to a whole section of ethics, or the do's and don't to live by.

We can credit the first written *yoga* guidebook to a man named Patanjali, who chose to write down the practice of *yoga* in his well-known book *The Yoga Sutras of*, wait for it, *Patanjali*. Hmm, no fucking ego there.

Anyway, in the *Yoga Sutras*, as they are most commonly referred to, we learn about these moral codes and ethical agreements called the *yamas* and *niyamas*. They are said to line the *yogi's* path so that he or she knows the right way to live. Are we finally getting to whether or not a *yogi* should or shouldn't say fuck? Maybe, just maybe. If I am boring you with all the backstory, please feel free to grab a cacao and acai berry snack and come back to me later.

Are you ready to dive into those *yamas* and *niyamas* now? Let's have a crack at it, shall we?

There are five *yamas*, typically known as ethical standards. They are:
- *Ahimsa* = non-violence
- *Satya* = truthfulness
- *Asteya* = non-stealing
- *Brahmacharya* - moderation or chastity
- *Aparigraha* - non-attachment

Ahimsa is the first ethical code that the *yogi* learns. To always practice non-violence, the *yogi* should never hurt another living being. This often leads the *yogi* to the acts of Vegetarianism or Veganism. I have always taught my students that our thoughts create our words and that our words culminate in our actions. Therefore, a deeper look into non-harming may lead one to the realization that any spoken word can potentially cause harm. This, of course, depends on what you are saying, how you are saying it, and who you are speaking to.

So if you are offended by the use of the word fuck, please know that it is not now nor ever will be my intention to cause you any harm. When I was younger, we used to say, "Sticks and stones may break my bones, but names will never hurt me." It meant not allowing any name-calling or verbal harassment to bother you. Living under the microscope of more recent years, however, it seems almost impossible to open one's mouth and not offend another to the point that there is a dramatic backlash. If we were to live long enough, we may see a day where we cannot say any words to another without creating some sort of tension. Perhaps that is why many ancient civilizations resorted to using symbols to communicate and why we seem to be moving back to them now (insert your favorite emoji here =   ).

Can we agree that dialogue is an important method of communication? And can we agree that because this is a two-party exercise, where language and experience can shape our individual understandings, sometimes this method goes wrong? Am I sometimes misunderstood? Yes. Do I sometimes speak without thinking? Didn't I already tell you that I was from New Jersey? But do I ever mean to hurt someone else by the things that I say? I like to think not.

Concerning *Ahimsa* and the use of the word fuck, it comes down to intention. If we are arguing and I say, "Fuck You!" out of anger, then I intend to hurt you. But if we are having a jolly time together, and you make a little joke about my pronunciation of the word "*Chakra.*" And by the way, it is not SHA-KRA. It never has been Shakra, it never will be Shakra, and it should never again be pronounced as Shakra. Notice that I didn't even use italics to reference it. If you are going to use the word, please say it correctly: CH, as in chalk; AK; as in clock; RA; as in the Egyptian God of sun, light, and life. What was I saying? Oh yes, imagine a fictional time when I might actually say *Chakra* incorrectly, and you poke fun at me. In our collective joy, I may say, "Fuck you." And when I do, we will both laugh and laugh and laugh. And there will be no harm done — unless you say Shakra. Then, all bets are off.

Satya means truthfulness. So, is saying fuck truthful? Yes. Sometimes, there is never a more truthful word or expression.

Asteya means not to steal. I'm going to go out on a limb and say that it does not apply here. But if you can think of a way, reach out. I'm everywhere, like holes in your husband's socks. Just my husband's? I don't think so.

Brahmacharya. Uh-oh. Houston, we have a problem!

Brahmacharya was originally translated to mean chastity. To be chaste, one would abstain from sexual intercourse. And I learned from watching *Risky Business* (a 1983 Tom Cruise movie, Millennials, Google it), about fuck, that if you can't say it, you can't do it. In all seriousness, the original definition of fuck is to have sexual intercourse. And, of course, saying and doing are not always synonymous.

For the ancient *yogis* who practiced chastity, it was to harness energy to be used for spiritual aspirations. These *yogis* were considered aesthetics because they abstained from all senses. They devoted their lives to the practice of *yoga*. They decided not to have families and went to live with their *guru* or in a cave and practiced *yoga* all day long, every day. It was total dedication to a belief that hinged on liberation being found through abstinence.

However...

There was also a sect of *yogis* called the *Tantricas* who said, "Well, I think liberation and bliss can totally be found through the senses!" Almost every single one of us reading this book live a more *Tantric* lifestyle than an Aesthetic one. Based on this, the translation of *Brahmacharya* can be meant as "Moderation." My Jewish Grandmother used to always say, "Anything in moderation." Well, I don't know about anything, but I do know that when she was watching the Philadelphia Phillies and they were losing, she did say the word fuck a lot. Ah. Maybe that's why my mother hates that word so much! This is a huge revelation here. I'm processing. Don't worry, you can keep reading, and it'll be like time never stopped. Unless you need to get a drink or go to the bathroom, in that case, go ahead. Let's both come back when we're ready.

Moderation in terms of *Brahmacharya* feels much more true to the essence, doesn't it? Being reverent concerning sex feels significant. Honoring your partner with love and loving acts is important. And, *Tantricas* consider the act of sex one of the most significant ones.

In my conclusion of *Brahmacharya*, I would like to add that in the previously aforementioned movie, *Risky Business*, it was the phrase "Sometimes you just gotta say 'what the fuck'" that got Joel into Princeton University. Enough said. You're wondering which streaming service you can watch the movie on, aren't you? I have it on VHS if you want to borrow it. Seriously, I do.

This leaves *Aparigraha,* or non-attachment. To this, I state, "What the fuck." This seems to define the usage completely and appropriately. It also segues nicely into the next section on the *Niyamas*:
- *Saucha* = cleanliness
- *Santosha* = contentment
- *Tapas* = purifying practices
- *Svadyaya* = study of spiritual scriptures
- *Ishvara-Pranidhana* = surrender to God

The only thing I am moved to say about these in respect to the word fuck is, isn't giving it up to your Higher Power, letting go, and trusting the Universe all the same as saying 'what the fuck?"

Take a moment. I'll wait.

In conclusion of the dissertation on whether or not a *yogi* could or would or should say fuck, I hereby declare a resounding Yes! Yes, a *yogi* can surely say fuck, albeit with the right intentions, and of course in moderation. Could I have wrapped this section up a while ago? Fuck if I know.

At least *Shiva* loves me.

Hey, while I am stirring the pot, I wanted to let you know that I will no longer italicize the word "yoga." It's just too much — right or wrong, it's just too much. While I'm at it, I will also discontinue italicizing the words yogi or yogini. Thank you for understanding.

I believe *Shiva* would also agree.

CHAPTER 2

I HATE THAT POSE

*"If cauliflower can become pizza,
then you can certainly do a handstand one day."*
~ *Unknown*

We've all been there, that moment in a yoga class when the teacher announces the next pose, and your mood dissolves from chill to not thrilled in a split second. You suddenly find that you need to take a sip of water, go into the Child's pose, or run out to pee — anything to avoid the cursed *Utkatasana* or whatever your unfavorite flavor is.

We all have a love/hate relationship with our *asana* practice. We are told by our teachers that our postures should all be firm and steady and that when we have an equilibrium of mind in the posture, we have found our "seat" and will be content to sit there in the pose, possibly indefinitely. Ah, but that just can't include the arms in Warrior 2, right? You know what I'm saying: you float the arms out straight and suddenly feel as though you've embodied the god Atlas and are carrying the weight of the world, represented by two large, overwhelming buckets full of iron being held in each hand.

Yoga postures, or *asanas,* have come to be what most people equate to all of *yoga* in our modern world. The over-focusing on the physical has led to an astonishing number of expert yogis on Instagram. It's as if they materialized out of nowhere, with little to no training, and self-proclaimed themselves to be at the top of their craft!

Hmm...

Since yoga's introduction to the West was credited to Sami Vivekananda, as introduced through demonstrations during the Chicago World's Fair in 1893, we've been captivated by the many calisthenics and gymnastics credited to the ancient yogis.

As an outwardly seeking, body-oriented society, we tend to focus more on the physical aspects of the being. As such, yoga *asana* is well suited for us Westerners who crave fit bodies that look good in our Calvin Kleins. Is that reference too dated? What type of jeans are the young folk wearing these days? Which Reality TV show personality has the newest TikTok out about them? Is TikTok still out there? This shit changes so fast these days that it's best to just look it up yourself. By the time this book gets out, whatever I write may be out of vogue.

According to statista.com, the cosmetic industry was set to top around 49 billion dollars in the USA alone in 2022[1]. With all the glorious filters out there, I'm not sure why everyone needs so much makeup anyway. With the click of a button, you can enhance your lips, give yourself mascara or eye shadow, and eliminate wrinkles. Well, whether it's real cosmetics or technologically enhanced photos, the focus on the external and the body in our modern-day world is more paramount to most people than other facets of our reality.

The pandemic of 2020 changed things for many yoga studios. My studio had been open for twenty years and was a staple of the Central New Jersey area. Even if someone had not practiced with me, they knew of the studio. While I watched many boutique studios open and close throughout the years, the longevity of my studio remained as solid a foundation as I could ask for. Suddenly, however, like many other yoga studios, I found myself in a difficult position at the end of the first quarter of 2020.

My beloved community, most of which had been with me for quite a while, was aging. Although new and sometimes younger people came in, most of my students averaged in their 50s to 60s, with some in their 70s. This "at risk" population no longer had an interest in coming into the studio to practice and, *Ganesha* forbid, breathe together in the same room. Our virtual classroom was working fine for them and me, so when it was time to renew my lease, I downsized considerably to a much smaller location around the corner.

Then the Universe said, "Just kidding, you can come out and play." It felt like as soon as I moved the studio to a smaller location, people wanted to come back inside and practice. Well, maybe 50% of them,

---

[1] https://www.statista.com/statistics/243742/revenue-of-the-cosmetic-industry-in-the-us/

anyway. The other half wished to stay home and log in. This created a hybrid situation that ultimately created the beginning of the end for me.

One thing that is difficult to convey to others is the amount of energy and attention that a good yoga teacher gives to their classes and students. If you are lucky, people will feel your compassion and your love for them and the practice, and they will continue to come to class month after month and year after year. A great teacher makes each one of her students feel just as important as the other, encouraging and nurturing in such a way that you, as the student, feel that you are receiving personalized guidance in a class that could be filled with twenty or more others.

In-person, there are ways to connect with your students that are much different than online. So when you navigate both at the same time, there is an exhausting level of attention to the most minute details to attend to everyone equally.

I have to admit that I tried my best and even heard from most people that my hybrid classes were much better than most others trying to do them. But to me, there was always something lacking. Rather than rant on about how I felt these classes were inadequate, it was March 2022, exactly two years into the bullshit that is Covid-19, that I decided to close One Yoga Center. Sitting in our home next to my husband, both sick with the virus and still attempting to get coverage for the few classes I was mustering up the energy to teach, I looked over at him and said, "I'm done. I'm closing the studio." And he turned his head and replied to me, "Okay."

And that was that.

Over the years, I have had so many amazing people come through the doors. I watched students transform through their *asana* practice. I remember the woman who used to come to the studio in the basement and cry night after night into her mat. I remember her thanking me for giving her that space and never judging her. I fondly recall the many teacher trainees that went through my training programs, some of whom went on to open their own studios.

And, I could always tell when someone was moving through a difficult phase in their life based on when they would walk back through my doors after several years away from the mat. The studio was more than a business, it was a refuge, a sanctuary, and a home for many people who thought that I would always be there when they needed me. But just like your practice changes over the years, so did this.

There was a time, I will refer to it as the "golden years," when I used to host these ridiculous three-hour power yoga classes that I called "Yoga Intensives." I would crank the heat up to 85 or 90 degrees (this was before anyone had infrared lights like the hot yoga studios of today), turn up the tunes on the CD player (before you had to pay a fee to play music in your classes), and call out *Samasthiti*! Then, for the next three hours, we would flow and sweat and laugh and push our bodies from one fatiguing sequence to another. Everyone loved them. It was a better workout than anything at the gym, and with mantras, meditations, and spiritually devised themes, we created meaningful practices.

Back then, I also had Dharma Mittra's "Master Chart of Yoga Asanas" laminated on my wall. Way before apps on your phone could crop out people and delete backgrounds with a push of a button, this wonderful yoga teacher sat and cut photos of himself in yoga postures with old-school scissors. This, what I can only imagine as a painstakingly grueling, process of fitting in 908 poses on one board, became a well-known fixture at many yoga studios. The beauty was to witness the fluid progression from a simple posture to the most complex variations. This poster would be my muse for many of these insane "Intensive" classes, as we would flow and grow together, allowing the postures to become more intense as we leveled up, *namaskar* after *namaskar*.

It is with certainty that I feel I was not the only teacher pushing her students to their physical limits in an *asana* practice. Not then, and certainly not now at the yoga *shala*. But somewhere along the way, my yoga practice changed, and I was forced to look deeper for a more meaningful practice than relying on more complicated *asanas* or sequences.

I have long said that injuries are our best teachers. When a teacher trainee cannot understand the need for instructing modifications in practice, I silently make a note to check back in with them after they have an injury themselves. It is impossible to teach a strong physical specimen the need to slow down and do less with his or her body. They cannot understand the concept. It's like telling an Olympic athlete not to go for the gold but that being at the Olympics is good enough. While it may be a nice sentiment, the athlete archetype needs to push himself to the maximum physical extreme — it's just in his DNA.

I have often found that my injuries have taken me to deeper places in my *asana* practice, not by pushing myself to work harder but by allowing myself permission to do less. Through breath, patience, and awareness, true healing can occur.

The ancient yogis recognized that the most difficult posture for any aspiring yogi was *savasana*, or the corpse posture, because it would require the student to be still in both body and mind. While most students love a good final relaxation after their hour of power, they are usually less enthused with a Yoga *Nidra*, or what is yogic sleep, practice without that *vinyasa* class predating it. It almost doesn't make sense to them. But when you find yourself in extreme pain, from say recovering from a burst appendix (oh, just wait til that chapter; that's a good story), you realize that the only thing you can do is lay there, breathe, and discover the energy in your body and how you are experiencing life at each moment.

While I do not wish injury on anyone, it is often the best teacher for any yoga practitioner. Moving in and out of postures, slowly and with extreme caution and reverence, is not only humbling but necessary in peeling back the many layers of the being, and not just healing but ultimately decoding one's True Self.

This seems a good place to plunk another golden nugget down from my teaching arsenal. For all the yoga teachers out there, please, for the love of *Ma Durga*, TEACH THE POSTURE. Don't just call out the name, assuming everyone understands what to do, even if everyone in the class is a "regular" student. Just do your job and teach the nuances of the pose with proper cueing. And yes, even for *Surya Namaskar*. The repetition of Sun Salutation leaves the body particularly vulnerable to injury — I've seen it a hundred times if I've seen it once. If your yoga teacher isn't teaching yoga poses every time, stop and ask them questions during class. They'll love that!

The yoga *asana* shit is powerful! In *Hatha* yoga, there is an underlying balancing act happening at every moment. The practice assists one in finding balance where one needs it. So, if you are inflexible in your hamstrings, you'll struggle with forward bends, and if your back is as stiff as a board, well, most postures will be difficult. Yet that's why we roll out the mat, right? So we can become more flexible where we are tight or tighten down the places that are too loose. Our yoga practices allow us this opportunity nicely, and over time, one can see much progress in these areas.

So, where are your weak spots? The body never lies. Tell me the issue in your tissue or the mess in your mind, and I'll tell you which pose you "hate." Let me know if I am close.

Weak Legs = Chair (*Utkatasana*)
Weak Arms = Warrior 2 (*Virabhadrasana 2*)
Tight lower back = Pigeon (*Adho Mukha Eda Pada Rajakapotasana* — I used to enjoy saying that one fast during teacher training programs to impress my students. How stupid.)
Stiff Back = Seated Forward Fold (*Pashchimottanasana*)
Weak Core = Upward Boat (*Navasana*)
Fear & Anxiety = Headstand (*Sirasana*)
Lack of Self Worth = Crow (*Bakasana*)
Tight Hips = Frog (*Bekasana*)
Inability to Sit Still = Final Relaxation (*Savasana*)
Unable to Focus = Balancing Postures
Neck Issues = Plow (*Halasana*)

Now that you've taken that little test, it's easy to see how everyone is going to have something that he or she is working on and, therefore, finds difficult in any *asana* practice. It's not only normal to have the challenges but quite typical to find yourself unhappy having to perform certain poses.

I have known many yogis who have gone out of their way to create really interesting excuses for how or why they don't practice certain postures when, in reality, you just need to be honest about it all. You know, there is a difference between "honoring your body" and simply copping out of working on a pose or its perfectly acceptable modification. Modifications are always the preference to exclusion.

In my yoga teacher training courses, I used to have my students sit in each *asana* that we discussed for five minutes. Then, the task was to write about the experience in the posture, and I do not mean just the physicality. It is easy to say, "Oh, I love Downward Dog because it is a great stretch for my whole body." While that may be true, it doesn't tell me what you felt in the pose. I want to know what emotions arose. I need you to discover your feelings when you sit and breathe through difficulty. And then, when you honestly can tell me that you "hate" the pose, great! We have just gotten somewhere in transforming not only your practice but also your life.

What happens on the yoga mat is always a reflection of what is happening in your life off the yoga mat. The postures are meant to create balance because we are meant to create balance in our lives. So when you figure out that you have a very strong dislike for Eagle Pose, then fantastic! Now, the work is practicing Eagle Pose, or an acceptable variation of it, every day. Keep coming back to the pose, keep breathing through it, and yes, keep hating it, at least until the feeling changes. But you can't bypass your way to creating balance, so you might as well accept the fact that you must do the poses you don't like even more often than the ones that you love. Because that is how change occurs.

One of my all-time favorite *yoga* quotes is from B.K.S. Iyengar, who said, "The pose begins when you want to leave it." That applies not only physically but also mentally. Notice where your mind goes in those postures. I will wager that when you dislike or are challenged by a pose, you do some of your best thinking while in it. P.S. Yoga is about stilling the mind stuff, remember. Do not be proud of this accomplishment.

But aside from the part about working through the tough postures, mindfully, there is another issue concerning this whole situation, and that is the use of the word "hate." That's right, yogis should never say hate, right? I mean, it's such a strong word for such gentle spiritual ahimsic warriors. Ahimsic? Is that a word? Well, not a Sanskrit one anyway; notice there are no italics.

I've had direct dealings with people who have a basic misunderstanding that those who practice yoga are or should be unemotional. This may come from the calm demeanor that most yogis appear to have after a yoga practice. But ask any true yogi and they will tell you that the whole reason that they practice yoga is so that they don't screw up the first *yama* by deploying violence against another who hath dost pissed us off. I mentioned this in chapter one already. Since it bears repeating, you may want to note it.

The reality is that our emotions are real and valid and that we need to feel and express them. This shows up in people who I find rigid in their body, as a whole, but especially in the lower back and hip area. Most times, I can unlock the stiffness in that area by simply showing people how to use the Surrender Breath while in a pose like Supine Pigeon, which can often turn into an audible emotional release, such as crying or laughing.

The subtle energy body anatomy teaches us that the second *chakra* in the sacral area is linked to our emotional identity. A healthy understanding of one's emotions, allowing oneself to feel, and learning how to appropriately express those emotions translate to an open flow of energy in this area of the body and, subsequently, greater ease in postures over time. Last time I checked, hate is a serious emotion, one that, say, a yogi may want to dive deeper into to understand their connection with.

I was taught never to use the word hate while growing up. I was also told, "Never say never." This created a bit of confusion, but luckily, I was able to understand where the sentiments were coming from. Although I do believe that my teachers had well-meaning intentions behind these statements, I am certain that the endless bottles of whiskey in their bottom desk drawers wouldn't have been necessary if they hadn't attempted to drown out their feelings for most of their lives. Did anyone else have drunken teachers growing up? Just Gen Xers? Now, all the teachers reading this hate me. I'm not talking about you, though. But please feel good about exploring those emotions that are being triggered.

If you practice yoga and you "hate" or severely loathe a pose, good. You just found your go-to practice that will bring about the biggest transformation for yourself.

To someone saying, "I hate this pose," if you are a yogi, I say go for it. Hate on it all day long. But work on it nonetheless, and soon you won't be saying that phrase anymore anyway. You'll have transformed that hate into love. Although I never advise using the achievement of a posture as your yoga "goal," the journey of getting there and what you will uncover through your body's intelligence will be worth all the struggle. Yoga is a practice, after all. Embrace it.

And while you do, *Ma Durga* will love you — especially if you get angry through it. She was born to thrive on that.

CHAPTER 3

WANNA HIT MICKEY D'S?

*"I was always a junk food person.
Still am."
~ Dolly Parton*

There is a lot to unpack in this chapter, and I am quite sure I am not going to be making any friends here very soon. So, let's have at it.

I believe that we can all agree that fast food or "junk" food is not healthy. Everyone knows it. Everyone accepts it. Yet, lots of folks still eat it. According to Grand View Research, a 2021 statistic states that the global fast food industry was expected to reach 593.3 billion

USD and is estimated to climb to 813.9 billion USD in 2028.[2] That's a lot of hamburgers, *Hanuman*.

The world has a love affair with fast food. It's true. If you ever have the opportunity to visit the Sphinx in Egypt, try to miss the McDonald's visible from the Giza Plateau. The fast food chains have moved into every corner of the globe, making them the first fully inclusive cultural food.

In 2009, I took my father back to Thailand for the first time since he was stationed there in 1968. We took a tour from Chiang Mai in the northern region, down through central Thailand and into Bangkok. We visited ancient ruins, witnessed how simple folks lived in the countryside, and explored many temples along the route. It was an extraordinary tour that solidified within me a strong love of the country and its culture, bodywork, and world-renowned food.

Thailand has ruined all my enjoyment of Chinese food. If I am going to have Asian cuisine, I will always get Thai food, or I will go without it. It's that good! Along our tour, we visited many fabulous restaurants but often encountered tour group buffets, which, after a while, seemed to be the same sort of dishes.

Not having the same enjoyment for Thai food as I, my husband was less than thrilled after a few days of Pad Thai and was craving "home" food. When we finally got to Bangkok and to our five-star hotel, both my husband and father couldn't wait to run across the street to McDonald's. They both said it was the most delicious hamburger that they'd ever had. I was more fascinated by the sundae with corn kernels on it. But I think I may have gotten the french fries. I'm a real sucker for the French fries.

---

[2] https://www.grandviewresearch.com/industry-analysis/fast-food-market

Another time, my friends and I were backpacking with a rail pass through Italy and had stopped in Rome. Now, Italian food is probably the most beloved cultural food around the world. And surely, being in Italy and enjoying the fresh gravies and the exquisite kinds of pasta and cheese was an experience to die for. I was in heaven. But on this one particular day, when we walked from one side of Rome to the other, and I was a big, sweaty, exhausted mess, I recognized the familiar golden arches on my tourist map and knew that I had to have it. Even in Italy, there was only so much Italian food I could eat.

Now, I know that some of you are grossed out and probably have lost some respect for me as a yoga teacher. I mean, we are supposed to work tirelessly on raising our vibration by purifying our bodies and minds. And while I choose to buy organic and have gone dairy-free and try to make the healthiest choices for myself most of the time, I enjoy a fountain Coca-Cola and Mickey D's from time to time — and I do not allow myself to wallow in guilt when I have it. I enjoy it, and then the craving is gone, and I move on to my goji berry and kale smoothies. Actually, that is a lie; I have never had a goji berry and kale smoothie. I don't even want to. But maybe you do. That's ok. I won't judge you, either.

Ah, but the dilemma is all about how we feed our bodies and whether fast or junk food can be considered energy. I will spare you the diatribe on *ahimsa* and not creating harm to another being, we went over that already. We know that anything harmful to another being should be avoided whenever possible. Yet, if we also read the *Bhagavad Gita*, we know that sometimes it is important to do your duty and even go to battle for just causes.

An animal rights activist will argue that there is no just cause for the killing and consuming of animals. As beings on the planet, all life is considered valuable. To a vegan, one should no more eat a pig than another human. Ah, but bacon! Really, can we have a pass on bacon? I'm visualizing *Arjuna* and his family on a battlefield, ready to go to war and needing nourishment to not only sustain them but to give them strength to persevere through the epic battles to come. I'm guessing that a light lunch of a spring salad with sprouts may not be the thing to get them through. If Jesus could turn water into wine, then *Krishna* might have materialized enough Pandi Curry to fortify his army. I think there's a *sutra* about that somewhere (people from New Jersey tend to lean towards a serious dose of sarcasm, in case you were wondering if I was serious).

We could spend more time here, but there is another bigger issue about food that I wish to explore: *pranic* vibrational energy.

When I teach yoga breathing or *pranayama* techniques in my training, we have to begin with a discussion of *prana*. *Prana* is simplified as "life force energy," the same as *chi* or *qi*. *Prana* is said to be in all living things, but more ample in sunlight, the oceans, food on the vine, and in anything we consider to be "alive."

To the ancient yogis, *prana* was a key to total liberation. To the modern-day yogi, *prana* should be considered for many reasons — from having good health to living a happy life. Understanding how to increase our *pranic* intake is significant and deserves a deeper look under the lens. In my training, we have lengthy conversations about how to generate more *prana*, and that lends to just how much *prana* exists in different foods.

Take, for example, that goji berry you love in your smoothie. I had to look it up, but apparently, they are goji berry farms in Northern California, even though the plant is indigenous to East and Southeast Asia and South Africa. So let's go with Northern

California as that is the closest to where I live on the East Coast of the USA, so, by default, you live there, too, in this example. Go with it.

Imagine that you wake up in Sonoma County, you walk into your backyard, which backs up to the goji berry farm, and you walk over to the plant, and you see a bunch of ripe berries ready for the picking. Before you snap one off of the shrubs, know that this is the most full of *pranic* energy that this little berry will ever have, still attached to the main plant, with roots in the dirt and branches growing up to the sun. Without hesitation, you rip off a few goji berries and plop them into your mouth. You are receiving that goji with as much *prana* as it can supply you. Way to go!

But remember, in reality, you don't live in Sonoma, California; you live in New Jersey. There is no goji berry farm in your backyard, and you have to drive to a local market for any goji berries. But, before you go to the market, realize that this plant doesn't grow there either; rather, it was trucked in from somewhere — in this scenario, we will go with California. The harvesting of the fruit took place, the berries sat in a barrel or bucket while all the others were being harvested, before they were cleaned and sold off to a company that would then package them and ship them off to all the grocery stores around the country, or in some cases, the globe.

How long did the goji berries sit in the bucket? How long did it take to package them? What was added to assist in the lengthening of their shelf life? Were they frozen and then defrosted? How long did it take for the lovely goji berries to travel from the packaging plant to your grocery store, where you took your time to read the package and ensure that you got the goji berries of the highest organic quality? And good for you, you made the best choice that you could at the store. But you know what? That goji berry doesn't have much, if any, more *prana* in it than your McChicken sandwich does now.

And what about vitamins and nutrients? While the harvested, frozen, and shipped avocado from California that I purchased with the goji berries (wait, you purchased, remember, it was you that wanted them in your smoothie) may have a different nutritional value than the cooked chicken sandwich, it still has just about the same amount of *pranic* energy flowing through it.

Or does it?

Everything that exists in the world vibrates at a unique frequency. This is true of what we would regard as "alive" as well as things not considered to be alive. Scientists can evaluate a substance's vibration in many ways, one of which is measuring the electromagnetic waves in food. By doing so, we can find out what types of foods have higher vibrations than others and thus understand which foods are best to eat to raise our vibrational frequency. Studies found that raw, fresh, and ripe fruit contains the highest vibration. No surprises there.

In an article by Lori A. Beyard for Clary Sage College, she states that foods with the highest frequency (6500-10,000 angstroms) are things such as fresh fruits and vegetables, whole grains, freshly laid eggs, white or green tea, etc. Cooked veggies, butter, honey, and cooked fish come in below that at around 6000-3000 angstroms. The bottom rung of food at 3000 angstroms is any processed or refined foods, sausages, cooked meats, chicken, pork, etc.[3] Okay, this is pretty good news for the fresh goji berry consumer in

---

[3] https://clarysagecollege.com/news/my-food-is-vibrating/

California, but it does lean toward validating my statement about the refrigerated, shipped goji berries on the East Coast.

Ayurveda, the Indian science often followed along with yoga, explores *prana* in foods to a great extent. According to *Ayurvedic* doctors, over-processed organic foods are not only devoid of *prana* but can harm the body, especially the gastrointestinal tract. And if any pesticides have been sprayed on the shrub, then you have a toxic chemical also being introduced, creating a worsening situation from your organically trucked special berries.

Yes, even organic foods, while typically healthier and better, can have a level of pesticides on them, especially if a neighboring farm sprays them. To clarify, the USDA does allow for certain pesticides that have met their requirements on organic food as of the writing of this book. However, RFK Jr. is now our Secretary of Health and Human Services, and he has a lot to say about many of these things. Hopefully, we will see some changes very soon in the quality of our food. But, remember, he was also photographed eating McDonald's with the President just before the election (I promise that is the last political reference in the book. I've never been a fan of it all, but I do think we all need to look at everything with our eyes wide open).

What does this all mean? Well, it means your Big Mac may have the same amount of *pranic* energy as your goji berries. For our *Ayurvedic* purposes, they are both dead and frozen or processed past the point of offering you any life force energy or nutrients.[4]

For those of us who live in the Garden State, we relish our veggie stands in the summertime. Oh, if you have never tasted a fresh Jersey Tomato sandwich in July, then you are missing a real treat.

---

[4] https://naya-ayurveda.com/ayurveda-and-organic-foods

Our fresh vegetables are some of the best, and it is nearly sacrilege to go into a grocery store in the summer to buy produce. Come winter, however, it is an entirely different story. We pretty much must get our food from the grocery store in wintertime in NJ, where nothing is fresh, and everything feels dead (that's why nearly half of NJ has moved to Florida for the winter). As I've already discussed, organic produce shipped from faraway places contains virtually no *prana* and minuscule nutrients.

I touched upon the concept of *pranayama* earlier in the chapter, but I want to dive in a tad (love that word "tad" — so cute). If *prana* is life-force energy, then the yogic breathing techniques of *pranayama* are said to increase the level of life-force within the human person when performed properly.

In the upper regions of India in the Himalayan mountains, where the ancient yogis used to migrate into caves isolating themselves away from the outer world to focus on the yogic practices and enter the inner world, it can be kind of nipply (That's a fun way of saying chilly. I enjoy visualizing hard nipples on the yogis. It reminds me that they're human). One would not expect to find fresh kale salads or Brussels sprouts growing in abundance in the northern regions. And just how much rice can a yogi eat?

With sensory withdrawal the fashion, yogis developed a method that sustained and enhanced life-force energy. In this way, they need not over-concern themselves with the fixation on nourishment from plants and other sources and discovered ample sustenance from the various *pranayama* practices. They even developed one, *Sheetali* breathing, that staves off hunger.

Today, modern science has confirmed the many positive health benefits of yoga breathing. But the ancient yogis determined this thousands of years ago without advanced technologies and just by becoming ultra-aware of energy at a microscopic level.

I have a strong feeling that the benefits and uses of *pranayama* practices will continue to grow and become more important in our increasingly discordant outer world where we find people retreating to their caves at an astonishing level to work from home, avoid unnecessary gas consumption, and support an erroneous feeling of safety from illness and stress. Like the yogis of yore, modern society is unplugging from the outer world in one way while plugging in more deeply in another way through the technologies of our digital age.

The pandemic created by the spread of COVID-19 in 2020 resulted in an epic surge in people staying at home. And while hunkering down was supposed to make people feel safer, reports from the WHO (World Health Organization) show that in the first year of COVID-19 alone, the global prevalence of anxiety and depression increased by 25%. We also know that heart-related issues, digestive disorders, obesity, and chronic pain are just the tip of the iceberg of physical ailments that can arise out of consistent issues of anxiety and depression.

My feeling about yoga, and particularly *pranayama* techniques, is that they should become regular everyday practices for everyone, as they are proven to counteract these other issues that have become prevalent in our health and well-being. Everyone, regardless of age or physical limitation, can practice some sort of yoga, and breathwork is the key to it all. Just like the aesthetics practicing yoga in the Himalayan caves, twenty-first-century yogis practicing yoga with Peloton will be able to increase their level of life-force energy within by consistent daily *pranayama* practice.

I find it best to teach pranayama properly in a therapeutic in-person environment. However, I downsized my home and don't have enough room for all of you now. I'm open to selling millions of copies of my book to purchase a much larger abode with a yoga pavilion where I can offer yoga classes. For this reason, please share my book with everyone you can. For now, the details here will have to suffice.

Initially, I begin teaching *yoga* breathing by inviting the practitioner to lie down on the floor and place their hands on the stomach area. Relax the muscles and start to take deep breaths in and out of the nose. When you are feeling more comfortable, exert pressure against your hands by pushing the stomach upwards when you inhale. It's like imagining that you are blowing air into a balloon and watching it expand. Try to hold the stomach full and up for a long pause, then start the slow exhalation, allowing it to slowly recede inwards and towards the ground. You'll want to repeat this "belly breathing" for several minutes or more if you can.

If you find this technique difficult, grab a bag of rice (don't have a bag of rice? Then go outside and fill a bag up with five pounds of dirt. Or drive to Aldi and grab a bag of rice. I'll wait…)

Now that you have the bag of rice, lie back down on the floor and place it on your stomach. When you inhale, try to push the bag up, hold it for a long pause at the end of the inhalation, and then start the slow exhalation. The weight of the rice or the bag of soil will give you enough resistance to work the diaphragm muscle and synchronize it back to the original blueprint.

Over time, you won't need the bag on your belly as you'll be able to sit up and perform the belly breathing in an upright position. When you get here, you can move on to other yoga breathing techniques widely used to help the yogi slow down the mind and increase pranic energy in the body.

Some of my go-to breathing techniques are:
- *Ujjayi* - I like to refer to this as the "ocean-sounding" breath. It not only helps improve focus and concentration, but it also brings an extra push of energy when I need it
- *Nadi Shodhana* - this is the alternate nostril breathing, which helps synchronize the hemispheres of the brain and creates a balance in the solar and lunar energies
- *4,4,8 or Kumbukha* - this counted breathing is perfect for those with overactive minds. Hi, Gemini brothers and sisters!
- *Bandhas* - use of the yogic "locks" are particularly good at enhancing the flow of pranic energy in the body. *Maha Bandha* refers to "the great lock" and is when the three main locks, Mula (root lock), Uddiyana (abdominal lock), and Jalandhara (throat lock), are performed together

Since there are many other yogic breathing techniques and tons of books and videos out there that explain them in detail, I will leave it to them for the lessons. However, I do recommend finding a knowledgeable teacher to guide you.

But as much *pranayama* as you practice, understand that it will not help your freeze-dried, packaged, and shipped goji berries one iota.

To make a long story short (that must be another Jersey saying), if you want to grab a Mickey D's or a Taco Bell or an Arby's, best do it at the time of year when your choice of foods with any *pranic* energy are at their lowest. Then, as long as it meets your personal dietary needs and restrictions, go for it. But all things in moderation, and make sure to have more goji berries smoothies than chicken fingers.

And remember, *Buddha* loves you, so remember to thank the animal or food before you consume it, like the Dalai Lama does. I read that years ago, so it must be true.

CHAPTER 4

DOES MY ASS LOOK FAT IN THESE LULULEMONS?

*"There are no grades of vanity;
there are only grades of ability in concealing it."
~ Mark Twain*

The song is running through your brain, isn't it? "You're so vain, you probably think this song is about you." Well, if it wasn't a moment ago, it is now. You're welcome!

Ah, vanity, a quality no humble yogi understands, right? How did you choose your yoga outfit? Did you look in the mirror before you left the house for class? Are you looking in the mirror at yourself during class? When you came up into Mountain Pose, did you fix your shirt? Don't pretend not to. Lying isn't very yoga-like. Be real. Everyone has a little vanity in them.

Ecclesiastes 3:19-20:
> "All is vanity. All go unto one place; all are of the dust and all turn to dust again."

The Bible quite literally tells us that we are all vain, even though in the end it doesn't even matter — wait, maybe I'm confusing that with the band Linkin Park. They've got a fantastic song *In the End* that says, "What it meant to me will eventually be a memory of a time when I tried so hard and got so far. But in the end, it doesn't even matter." Sing it with me! Okay, maybe we will talk about yogis who listen to alternative rock later. For now, let's get back to vanity.

I've known lots of yogis who claim that they eat right, exercise, and practice yoga solely to increase their vibration and to live a longer and healthier life. You can't hear it, but I just put my hands over my mouth and made a farting noise. Now you hear it, right?

I am not debating the original premise or reasons why people would want to be healthier and take better care of themselves. I am stating that once you get a look at yourself twenty or so pounds lighter, you are most definitely going to notice, and you are absolutely going to like the way that you look. That, my friends, is called being human. And Yahweh still loves you.

This being human thing has caused us a bit of trouble. There are lots of people who have gravitated towards the saying, "We are all spiritual beings having a human experience." But I challenge that we could also as easily say we are human beings having spiritual experiences. I mean, the fact is that we are human beings. We may have originated from stardust, and we know that the layers of our being exist well beyond our understanding of the physical and mental parts of ourselves, but at least right now, in this lifetime, we are all human beings.

I believe that we once began as a part of the One Being, and in the reality system of Oneness, we lived a beautiful, harmonic existence. Then, we got the bright idea to come to Earth and birth this same truth here on this planet but in human bodies. When we split apart from the One Being and began our descent down into material form, our memory of Oneness faded quickly, and what we were left with has been the predominant reality system on earth: duality, which thrives off of our individual ego-based human experience.

The ego is the part of the human being that keeps us feeling as if we are separate units of consciousness, which we are on one very basic level. We find ourselves now, in this time, in the midst of reclaiming our Oneness in human form — something that has never been done before.

In this New Earth, many of the duality-based systems, like governments, banking institutions, and religion, are all beginning to crack apart. More people are seeing the holes in what we previously felt were the foundations of our reality here on Earth. As more people awaken to reclaim our Oneness, we will see many more shifts happening to alleviate the cycles of *karma* and suffering that we humans have managed to wrap ourselves all up in. But for now, we still have to live in a time when this is all playing out.

Deep stuff and difficult times we find ourselves in, hmm. If you just heard Yoda saying that, you're my people.

I believe that the ancient yogis saw the truth of who we are and, in their highest human form, tried to cultivate methods for us to get back to our true essence.

The methodology of yoga is one of the best practices today that I know that gives us so many techniques and philosophies to help us live in human form as best as we can. And like a good Jewish mother, they were really, really good at pointing out our shortcomings — for our own good and self-development. I know this because I'm half-Jewish. Okay, a quarter, but it was my mother's mother, so to that side of the family, I'm all Jew. Don't tell the Methodist priest on my father's side who Baptized me.

If we go back to *Patanjali's Yoga Sutras* for a moment, we uncover another layer of yogic philosophy that assists us in understanding the origins of all of our problems. The *kleshas,* or causes of suffering, are broken down. Some years later, the Buddha would also further dive into the causes of suffering in his details for the Four Noble Truths.

Continuing on the yogic path, and listed in order so that you may obsess about them more deeply, are the *kleshas*:
- *Avidya* = ignorance
- *Asmita* = over-identifying with your ego
- *Raga* = attachment
- *Dvesha* = repulsion
- *Abhinivesha* = attachment to life, fear of death

In *Sanskrit*, the language of yoga (that's what all these italicized words are in the book), *klesha* translates to poison. According to *Patanjali*, these five poisons keep humans away from truly experiencing life as blissful. Instead, they cause us pain and suffering. And, yes, they are each something that we all deal with in our lives. The *kleshas* turn up to show us where our work lies. If we acknowledge them, then we can begin this somewhat arduous task of working through them. For this, we go back to the *yamas* and *niyamas* for assistance.

I'll give you a little yoga story representing each of the *kleshas* so that you can understand them better. It'll be fun — unless, of course, you identify too much with one of the stories. In that event, grab a box of tissues and your journal, pause the reading to feel it, and jot it down. Remember that your emotions are real, and you can learn a lot from them. After that, pull up your big girl (or boy) panties, and let's get on with it.

Story #1: Ron is a tabla player for your favorite local *kirtan* band. Ron is well-liked by everyone who attends the chanting sessions at the yoga *shala*. But Ronnie has a warped sense of reality. He has convinced himself that by choosing the path of abstinence and honing his tabla playing craft, he is storing valuable *pranic* energy, increasing his overall life capacity, thus rendering an immortal life.

While the first part of this may have some validity, the dude seriously believes his body will never, ever, ever die. He is obsessed with doing everything he can to increase his *prana* for a long life and has, in doing so, lost out on many potentially loving relationships with a significant other. He justifies this by reminding himself that nobody else will live as long as he does anyway, so why waste the time getting involved? We can say that Ron suffers from *Avidya*.

Story #2: Chad, the new yoga teacher at the yoga *shala*, is a real hottie — and he knows it. He came into his first yoga class clad in only a speedo and his 8-pack abs, and it was a *yin* class. During the practice, you catch Chad checking out his abs in the mirror. When he notices you spying on him, he winks, smiles a flirty little gaze, and strokes his blond locks with his fingers. You put your head down, smiling, feeling all things, Chad. Then, about five minutes later, when you can no longer avoid the chemistry between you, you peek up again, only to witness Chad having a similar exchange with Yolanda, the new girl. When Chad sees you catching him, he winks at you, at her, and ensures that you both understand that he can easily accommodate both of you. *Asmita* may as well have Chad's picture next to it.

Story #3: Jane loves crystals. From the first time she found a quartz point hiking on a family vacation at seven, Jane has loved the shiny, sparkly gems. Her love affair with crystals continued as a young adult when she stumbled upon the various new-age shops in Sedona. Before she knew it, Jane was grabbing crystals from Instagram retailers every Wednesday and Friday evening and from Facebook retailers on the weekends. At this point, Jane has enough crystals in her inventory to open up a retail shop — if only she could bear to part with them.

Every morning, Jane chooses which crystals to place in a small material bag and stash in her bra for her day. The various wire-wrapped pendants in her jewelry box also get hand-selected each morning, depending on the type of energy she needs for the day or what colors she is wearing. Sometimes, she even coordinates both of these things.

On the times when Jane goes on vacation, she has to sort through which crystals to take with her. Crystals are Jane's most prized possessions, and all she can think about is what more she needs to have. She even has an expensive insurance policy out on them. Jane is so attached to her crystal collection that it takes up most of her extra time and energy. Wow, I feel a lot like Jane in this scenario.

Story #4: Babette dislikes being at the front of the yoga room. She usually attempts to arrive early enough to get a good spot in the back, where she can try to hide from most of the teachers. But more often than not, it seems that she gets stuck in traffic on the way from work to yoga and is forced to be in the front for all to watch her sloppy practice and inability to hold postures as long as she should be able to.

Each time she is stuck in the front, she simply cannot concentrate, which, of course, confirms a self-fulfilling prophecy that she does not have a good yoga practice. She then drives home, biting her lip and judging herself for not doing better. Babette's aversion to being in the front of the room continues to create a great amount of unnecessary suffering for her.

Story #5: Nobody wants to die. We may not always love our life, but we do not want to die. Yet everyone is going to die, including Ron, our tabla player. Someone should tell him. The notable *Sanskrit* scholar Georg Feuerstein once said that, from his understanding, the mortality rate is still 100%. He's been dead for a while, but he's still right, and someday, each of us will join him. But until then, we all want to live the best life that we can live. Being wrought with fear of death is no way to live.

We do an exercise in my teacher training about fear. I ask each trainee to write down his or her biggest fears. Then, pick any one of them to work with. Let's say you have a fear of snakes. Snakes get a really bad rap. I blame the authors of the Old Testament who wanted us to be a fearful lot — even though God specifically tells us to "fear not." But then again, he also told us to fear him. If you want to learn a lot about fear, pick up a copy of the first edition and dive in. Anyway, no matter what one's fears are, you can break each one down to the fear of death.

Going back to the poor snake, you start with the subject of your fear and keep asking, "And what is the worst thing that can happen…" until you get to the big one.

Example:
If a snake were to pop up in front of me, what's the worst that could happen? I can get bit. And if I get bitten by a snake, what's the worst that can happen? I can die. See how quickly that one worked out? Use this for any fear, rational or irrational, and you will eventually get to the dreadful death card. Once you are there, you can begin to scour your misunderstandings about death and reconcile that spiritual self and what happens there.

Einstein was quoted as saying that, everything being energy, the energy never ceases to exist; it only changes form. Many spiritual traditions believe in reincarnation. So whether you believe in science or Spirit, it's all the same here: there is no death when it comes to your true essential nature. And yet, all the humans on the planet, nearly 8 billion of us, all fear death, or at least we do until we reflect on this *klesha*. Then, we just don't want to be in any pain when we die. Or is that just me?

Well, as luck would have it, the ancient yogis developed a technique to assist with these pesky *kleshas*: *pratyahara*, or sensory withdrawal. For modern yogis, the understanding of *pratyahara* is either quite misunderstood or neglected entirely. In our ladder of the Eight Limbs of Yoga — oh wait, I haven't mentioned that yet. That's what *Patanjali* called the "eightfold path" to yoga. Sorry, I can sometimes omit the details. Ask any of my students how many spelling errors are commonly found in my training manuals. Anyhoo, in the Eight Limbs, we climb through *yamas* and *niyamas*, *asana* and *pranayama*, which all feel mostly tangible, and get to withdrawing of the senses and find ourselves hitting the breaks a bit. And we probably should, because shit gets real here.

Pratyahara takes a serious internal banking, requiring an enormous concentrated effort to attain a continued space of releasing the outer fixations of attachment, repulsion, ego, and ignorance. All of the *kleshas*, you see, are spawned from seeking outside of ourselves. So, for the yoga practitioner, *pratyahara* becomes an extremely important step in achieving the liberated state that we desire to have.

How do we do it?

Well, I suppose the first step is to turn off your mobile device and perhaps shut down your social media accounts. Then maybe you can try spending a full day in quiet, by yourself, out in nature, without your Apple watch, and figure some shit out. Then do it for a month or more until the endless nervous energy subsides, your vibrational energies shift into a higher octave, and you are truly ready to accept the unbroken attainment of sensory withdrawal. No? Well, maybe just an hour of power at the yoga *shala* for a quickie version, then?

Understanding the *kleshas* on a deeper level, we can consider their connection to vanity. The one common thread amongst all the stories and the *kleshas* is that ever-so-human quality or identification: ego. Ignorance, attachment, aversion, and fear of death all occur at times in our lives because human beings have egos. And with ego comes the somewhat misguided understanding that we are the center of our own universe, our own individual unit of consciousness, spiraling through life on a journey unto ourselves.

I can already hear some of you silently whispering, "Wait, but I am."

Nope, Twinkle-Toes, you are most certainly not.

We often refer to the ego as our "false self." It is the ego that identifies us as the many masks that we wear throughout our lives, such as a yoga teacher, a mother, an advanced yoga practitioner, a brother, a fireman, an attorney, a good *yogini*, a potty-mouthed author, etc. And since the ego can create this false sense of being separate, creating tons of obstacles to our capacity of being truly happy, then do we care what our ass looks like in a set of yoga leggings?

Yes. Yes, we care how we look.

We have always cared about how we look because it is a reflection of who we think we are, even for those of us who understand this to be an illusory method of thinking. It may not matter what others think of us, but we always have an opinion about ourselves.

That is human nature.

That is ego.

To deny our ego self is to deny our humanity. And humanity does come with some pretty cool stuff, too.

For one, I am a huge fan of standing upright. Right now, as I write this book, I am digging the ability of creative expression. And each one of us on the planet, every 7.888 billion of us, has our own unique fingerprint, DNA, and, according to current technologies, facial recognition. Although, I have my concerns about that last one. What about twins? Or triplets? And what about the many Elvis doppelgängers out there? Well, at least we have our fingerprints.

So being unique and individual is kind of cool, too. Of course, we strive to connect to the web of Oneness and to move into the Unity-Consciousness that is at hand. But we take on that task while inhabiting our human bodies. And all human bodies do one day die. And darn it, that means that the Bible was right.

Thankfully, Yahweh loves us!

We are lucky to be living in a time of body positivity, where everyone should enjoy a positive body image regardless of popular culture's ideas of what that is. The fact that many people still do not harken to what I am simply stating: it is our ego at play providing the suffering through the judgments that we take on about ourselves. We are now and will always be our own worst critics.

In addition to *Shiva, Ma Durga,* Buddha, and Yahweh, I love you. And, in conclusion, remember that black is a slimming color.

CHAPTER 5

NAMASTE

"It is also said that in bowing down before Buddhas, there is actually nobody to bow down to and no one bowing. Who bows to what? In truth, nobody bows to anyone, and yet there is this wonderful, free, gratitude-filled bowing down. In this subjectless, objectless, wholehearted bowing, nothing is excluded. The whole world bows. All creatures - men, women, animals, insects - bow to one another in mutual greeting. Is this not true thanksgiving?"
~ Roshi Philip Kapleau

In the 1990s, when I first started practicing yoga, my teacher placed her hands together in a prayer-type position at her heart, bowed her head, and said the phrase *"Namaste."* I did not know what it meant, but the beautiful sound filled my heart, and so I mimicked her, placed my hands at my heart, and bowed my head in return.

It took me a while to say the word back because I honestly didn't know what the fuck it meant or why I was doing it. It was such a foreign custom to me, and I did not want to do anything inauthentically. Flash forward twenty-five years later, and there has rarely been a time in a yoga class when, as a teacher, I did not put my hands in *Anjali Mudra*, bow my head, and say *Namaste*, except for the classes I teach in places such as treatment centers where it is important to be trauma-informed. Other than that, it has become a part of me as a yoga teacher.

Often translated as "The light in me honors the light in you," this simple word has been under quite a lot of scrutiny in today's world. Some squeaky wheels think that the use of *Namaste*, especially at the end of a yoga class, is an inappropriate use and blatant cultural appropriation, and they are getting a lot of headlines. But just what is cultural appropriation? Where are the boundaries between what is polite and respectful and what is an egregious adaptation of another's culture? And who gets to decide this?

I have a difficult time with the new hard lines about cultural appropriation. The phrase itself did not exist before the 1980s, but then again, we were still fighting the acknowledgment of racism at that time.

Sometimes, we need to accept the limitations and wrongdoings of the past to heal energy and move forward in a positive direction. I get that. And even though I like to believe that I am always being respectful, apparently others have different feelings about this that do require a little self-inquiry if I am to be a responsible member of society — although most days I'd rather be the Fairy Queen of the forest. I'm fairly certain I am already of Fae descent anyway, but that is a whole other story. I believe I could write a lot of other books on these and other fascinating topics. For now, I should probably just focus on this one.

As an Interfaith Minister, I find the whole line of inquiry regarding cultural appropriation incredibly challenging. I am tasked to incorporate significant aspects of different faiths into meaningful ministries whilst not adopting cultural practices and erroneously using them for my own purposes. And there's no good guideline for any of it, although many will try to impose them on you if you allow them.

When I was attending a holistic massage school, one of my fellow students, Ocie, was married to a Lakota elder named Bear. We would visit Bear, bring him gifts of tobacco, and he would talk to us about and teach us Lakota traditions. We were invited to take these traditions on and into our lives because the Lakota wanted us to understand their ways of living in harmony with nature. Thus, I learned how the art of smudging with white sage was taught correctly and brought into my everyday world, often teaching others today.

Using the smoke of ceremonial white sage, I often clear energy in my home, work, or on my person., Today, many frown upon a white woman using sage, calling it cultural appropriation. But what I think is that people don't even understand the meaning of their own words.

The Oxford Dictionary states of cultural appropriation:
> "the unacknowledged or inappropriate adoption of the customs, practices, ideas, etc. of one people or society by members of another and typically more dominant people or society."

First of all, I've always acknowledged the original Native Americans for the use of white sage for smudging. When lighting sage to smudge, I give thanks to the culture that brought us this practice.

Secondly, I use sage exactly as was taught to me by both Bear, who was of Lakota descent, and my original yoga teacher, who was also part Cherokee Native American.

Thirdly, as a woman, I can't be considered a "dominant people" since women worldwide struggle for equal rights to our male counterparts. Don't even get me started. It's another book for another time.

Finally, there is my title of Interfaith Minister, where I've been given the privilege of bringing in the use of smudging to any of my rituals and practices, where appropriate. We can safely say that using sage correctly is not cultural appropriation. The same goes for the use of *Namaste*. So unless you know who the people are and how they are using sage, you have no right to accuse anyone of such a thing.

The second line of issue that people have taken concerning saying *Namaste*, and even to the entire practice of yoga, is in regards to the origins of the practice and the larger issue of whether or not yoga constitutes as being a religious practice that should only be accepted by those of that particular religious sect.

The commonly accepted lineage of yoga is that the practice originates in India, as already mentioned, and that the word *yoga*, like *Namaste*, is *Sanskrit*.

Sanskrit, being the root language of many other Indian languages, is often accredited to being of Hindu origin. However, the truth is that the first evidence of *Sanskrit* use is not from India, but from

Syria, in the 2nd Century BCE. At that time, the ruling dynasty, the Mittani, who spoke another language, used *Sanskrit* names for their kings and other elite members of society. They even honored the same gods as in the *Rig Veda* and have the oldest document of a horse-training manual in the world using many other *Sanskrit* words.[5]

I guess this little tidbit of information puts a little kink in the shorts of the arrogant snot-nosed yogi influencers throwing around their trendy accusations at their parents and others of their generation who find true reverence in bowing and proclaiming, "*Namaste.*" Should we tell them? Never mind, they're already onto the next important thing. But just in case, let's school them some more.

Yoga comes from the root "*yuj*," which means to join or integrate. Yoga is said to mean "to yoke." A yoke is a wooden crosspiece that fits over the heads of two animals that pull an object like a cart. Together, the animals must work to pull the cart evenly. Yoga is, therefore, a practice where we bring together all the pieces of our being to join all the pieces of all the beings in Oneness. It is a practice of understanding who we truly are at our core essence.

While postures are a part of the yoga practice, the exercises and calisthenics that most have defined as yoga are an egregious misunderstanding of the totality of what yoga is. Exclaiming, "I'm going to practice yoga," is incorrect. "I practice yoga *asanas*" would be a better phrase. "Yoga kicked my *asana*," while cute and personally identifiable, is also not appropriate, classically speaking — although now I want that on a t-shirt.

---

[5] https://scroll.in/article/737715/fact-check-india-wasnt-the-first-place-sanskrit-was-recorded-it-was-syria

Nobody actually knows the true origins of yoga. Ask any yoga teacher how old yoga is, and you will get a different answer or a blank stare. We do understand it to be at least 5,000 years old due to some cave drawings in the Indus Valley area. Yoga is also listed in the oldest Hindu text, *The Rig Veda*, written around 1500-1000 BCE, although, again, those dates will change depending on what source you read. Nobody actually knows the exact dating of the book, and nobody knows the full origins of what was finally written down, as these and other yogic scriptures are derived from a vast oral tradition.

Many believe the traditions of yoga to be more like 10,000 years or older but cannot cite any concrete examples recognized by mainstream historians or archeologists. Therefore, the word yoga, being of *Sanskrit* origin and found in the oldest text from the Indian subcontinent, is given to belong to the vast Hindu tradition.

This formality has given rise to the long-running argument questioning yoga as a religious or spiritual practice. Scholars, historians, and yogis continue to debate this idea today. And there are quite decent arguments for both sides. I've already mentioned why many people feel yoga is of Hindu origin. But I've also provided some arguments against them too. When it comes to the premise of any knowledge, I go back to my favorite quote from Socrates, who said, "The only true wisdom is in knowing you know nothing." No matter what academics and other smart people like to debate, to the complete and utter confusion of myself, this always helps me feel smarter. Besides, based on this sole quotation from an ancient Greek philosopher, I am a genius.

There's also an episode of *Friends* that I love to quote regarding man's egotistical viewpoints on what is proven scientific factual evidence. In this episode, Phoebe argues with Ross over the validation of Evolution. As a scientist, he throws "facts" at her throughout the episode.

The episode continues something like this (and I apologize to *Friends* if I butcher this. Let me know, and I'll retract it in person on the next reunion special):

Phoebe: Wasn't there a time when the brightest minds in the world thought the world was flat? (Ross grins)

Phoebe: And that up until about fifty years ago, you all thought that the atom was the smallest thing until they split it open, and this whole mess of crap spilled out. Now, are you telling me that you are so unbelievably arrogant that you won't admit that there's a teeny, tiny possibility that you could be wrong about this?

Ross: (After pausing to reflect) There might be a teeny, tiny possibility

And just like that, the quirky massage therapist beats the scientist at his own game.

Isn't that a beautiful reminder to stay humble and remove arrogance and egoism from our viewpoints? How can we truly know the truth when, over time, "facts" change with our growing awareness?

As for what we know about yoga, we can consider that while ancient yogis may have been the first ones to write down the practice of yoga, the origins could come from an even older or ancient civilization that either chose not to write them down or whose entire existence has almost been obliterated.

To this point, I find the work of journalist and author Graham Hancock to be incredibly interesting on this subject matter. On his website, he hosts an author of the month, and this is where I found author David Frawley. His December 7, 2008 post on Hancock's site titled "Ancient Yoga and Shamanism: Yoga and Tantra" indicates that Shamanic practices dating back to the Ice Age show indications of ancient yogis being present in them.[6] This, of course, opens up the discussion of the real origins of yoga.

We also have evidence of the *Sanskrit* language being used in Syria before being established in India, which also supports, through historical evidence, that we may not understand its true origins. If we cannot agree on the age and can leave space to question the origins of the practice of yoga, we cannot, therefore, allow it to be possessed by Indians or Hinduism.

Hey, what if Hindus appropriated yoga from someone else? To most of today's practitioners, that comment might top off the list of shit yogis shouldn't say. But it's out there now. I'm not taking it back. Let it soak in.

Even if we want to keep yoga's origins with Hinduism, can we say that to practice yoga means that you have to be Hindu or subscribe to Hinduism? The short answer is, absolutely not. Tibetan Buddhists founded their Five Tibetan Rites some 2500 years ago. Translated as the "Fountain of Youth," the Five Tibetans consist of five yoga exercises performed several times a day. Buddhism is an entirely different spiritual tradition than Hinduism, and yet Tibetan Yoga is quite popular and an accepted tradition all over the globe.

---

[6] https://grahamhancock.com/phorum/read.php?8,983246,983246

According to the International Yoga Federation, as of January 2022, 300 million people around the world practice some form of yoga.[7] So are 300 million (minus those who follow Hinduism in India, I suppose — and, by the way, you do know only about 80% of the people in India practice Hinduism as a religion, leaving 20% of Indians to honor other religious practices, right?) people subscribing to cultural appropriation? Well, if so, at least they aren't all saying *Namaste*! Or are they?

Ah, the endless debate of territorial domination. It feels like a couple of un-neutered male dogs having a pissing match. We might be able to debate endlessly, depending on how much energy you have for it. But I just keep coming back to the concept behind bowing to one another, in deep and true reverence, and acknowledging the pure energy of one another in our complete whole form. Remind me why this is wrong.

When I travel throughout Thailand or Bali, which I have done extensively, the use of bowing is done in both greetings and goodbyes.

In Thailand, placing the hands at the heart, bowing, and saying "*Sawadee-Ka*" (for women, *Sawadee-Krup* for men) is customary and promoted as being appropriate for tourists and visitors to use.

In Bali, the traditional greeting is placing the hands at the heart, bowing, and saying, "*Om Swastyastu*."

The Japanese also bow and have different greetings depending on the time of day or situation, but perhaps the best known is "*Konnichiwa*," meaning "Hello."

---

[7] https://disturbmenot.co/yoga-statistics/

Most Asian countries have a form of greeting etiquette that includes bowing and the use of a word that would be foreign to anyone else.

Although the actual words change, instead of being upset by my bow and the butchered pronunciation of their language, the people respectfully smile and happily accept this as appropriate. They may attempt to teach me the correct articulation, and they should. But they opt to encourage me to adopt their kind and gracious practice. Because of this, I have always felt comfortable including it when I have the opportunity.

Just like Bear, many moons ago, when the intention is to teach others the ways and customs of the elders and ancestors so that more people can come together in loving ways, bowing to one another is a fabulous tradition to not only admire but bring into one's life.

And when I, as a yoga teacher, use this greeting or closing, I am confident that all of the yoga teachers and yogis before me are with me when I bow to my students. The long lineage — no matter where the origins derive from — is strong with one who connects with such reverence and consistency.

As a yoga student, it is more disrespectful to not reciprocate the bowing and use of *Namaste* than it would be to ignore your teacher's attempt to connect. And when a yogi meets another yogi at the local coffee shop and shares a little "*Namaste*" there, that's fine too. A yogi would share this because a yogi understands the loving intention behind the word and the salutation.

And remember, saying *Namaste* affirms that Great Spirit loves you.

For those keeping track, so far, we have covered the following yogic ideas and principles:

>Types of Yoga
>*Yamas/Niyamas*
>*Asana*
>Body/Mind Connection
>*Prana*
>*Kleshas*
>*Pratyahara*

Those are quite a few aspects of yoga. I hope that you're enjoying the conversation and maybe even learning a few things along the way. In hindsight, I should have titled this my "Master Class" on Yoga! And I definitely should have charged more. Shit!

One of the things that I have always admired about the yoga practice is the way that it constantly unfolds. I am always a student, learning and growing. Well, ideally, I want to stop growing. Once you hit menopause, that word takes on a whole different meaning. However, I commit to continuing to be an ongoing student of yoga and the world.

I'm sure that you have heard the onion metaphor already, but for those who haven't, I'll sprinkle it in for ya. An onion has many hidden layers. Looking at an onion on the outside, one has no idea how many layers are on the inside. The yoga practice is like that. You start with postures, breathing, or meditation techniques. But as you go along and the months turn into the years, you realize just how complex this ancient practice is and that its sticking power lies in its ability to continue to astonish you in the ways that you are, indeed, unlearned. Yoga is a deeply humble practice. And to anyone out there who professes to fully understand it, give me an hour on the mat with you.

Wow, that got a little strong, didn't it?

It doesn't matter; *Wakan Tanka* loves us all.

CHAPTER 6

MY THIRD EYE IS BLOCKED

"I've been thinking with my guts since I was fourteen years old, and frankly speaking, between you and me, I have come to the conclusion that my guts have shit for brains."
~ *Nick Hornby, High Fidelity*
(played by fellow Gen Xer, John Cusack),

Ah, the ever-popular yet so-elusive 3rd-eye! Just what is it, and why do so many aspiring yogis put so much energy and effort into opening it up? And what if yours just won't work? Maybe it's broken. What if you are Third Eye Blind? (My sincerest apologies to the members of the band for this "Dad" pun; it just came out.)

Back around 1998, my girlfriend and I traveled to the great, secluded, and vast wilderness of Massachusetts to seek out a woman our yoga teacher had touted as a psychic intuitive with very special gifts that we just had to have a session with. At this time in my life, I would try any new age/spiritual endeavors to figure out my life. I was still working full-time in a corporate office, was in a poor relationship, and felt stuck in my life just about everywhere.

Yoga and my first teacher had opened my eyes to many other realities, and I was on a mission to figure out what would bring me true happiness. The Massachusetts Mystic sounded like a fine idea, and besides, I always enjoyed a good girl's trip with my good friend.

My girlfriend had her appointment first while I sat downstairs in this woman's home, impatiently awaiting mine. In usual fashion, my friend had a fabulous reading and was beaming from ear to ear about what the psychic had told her. I couldn't wait to experience the same thing. Yet, again, in my usual fashion, my experience was quite the opposite of my friend's.

It was not long into the reading when the woman asked me to close my eyes and go into my third eye. A deep feeling of inadequacy immediately set in. Couldn't she just tell me what was going on? Wasn't that what I was paying her for? Why was she putting me to work? Maybe she should be paying me!

Well, suffice it to say, about a minute into her trying to have me open my third eye, she was jumping up and splashing cold water on it, alerting me to what I already knew: mine was blocked. She had guided me to close my eyes and envision a window and asked me what I saw when I looked inside. Seeing blackbirds was not a good omen to her, although I would tell any of my students today that this was a tremendous start to awakening their intuition. But my visions of blackbirds upset the woman.

Frankly, I am a bit upset with her, too. Now, I understand from Bear, my Lakota elder friend, that ravens and crows are spirit guides that assist in opening one's intuitive and clairvoyant abilities.

The Norse also understood this very well, as the "all-father," Odin, had two ravens who symbolized his power to see into the future. I'm not sure what her background was, but the woman I am calling the Massachusetts Mystic obviously hadn't a clue how significant seeing blackbirds was.

Although at the time I felt severely incapable, I now see how her reaction to my third eye's visions created a flow of disempowerment of my abilities for many years. For a long time, I repeated the mantra she provided me with: "My third eye is blocked." It's okay. I took my power back a long time ago, and I have long forgiven myself and her. I am happy to report that my third eye is open today, and I have instilled many checks and balances to ensure that I do not float up and away in its energies.

However, this inability to accept my intuitive abilities continued for many years. While my other yogi friends seemed to be "open" so much more open than I (having cool visions in meditation, experiencing trance states of consciousness through movement exercises, and channeling various ascended masters in Reiki sessions) I was confused about what this mystical power was or how to get it. At one point, I simply resolved myself to the fact that I may never have the same skills as others, and that was okay.

Years went by, and yoga teacher after shamanic practitioner would divulge the many layers of intuitive understandings that they continued to unearth during meditations, healing sessions, and astral travels. Many would ask my opinions about their visions or if I saw the same. I dared not tell them that I had no freaking idea because I had little to no visions. I mean, no yogi would admit to having a blocked third eye, right!? Well, now you know.

I shut down because I was told by the Mass Mystic and also by my yoga teacher that my third eye was blocked. So I believed them, at least until the one day I started to have my mystical awakenings.

Maybe it was through my many years of yoga practice, or perhaps that need to unlock this dreaded third eye, but I found a key that is so simple it escapes many other people, too. My problem, you see, was my big Gemini mind, all the constant mental activity, and the inquisitive nature of needing to understand by continually thinking things through. Yoga truly assisted me in relieving this constant internal banter. I even healed terrible insomnia through yoga practices, and now I sleep like a baby after a bottle of warm milk. Not the peeing-in-my-sleep part, but you get the symbolism.

The simple skill came to me during a workshop on developing your psychic abilities. The cool thing about owning a studio is that you can bring in anyone you want to instruct their workshops, and then you get to take them yourself. So, I knew a woman who was a medium that I felt pretty confident with at the time, and I brought her in to teach this one-day course.

I was paired up with another student of mine for the activities and was struck with an awful feeling of dread. Immediately, I took on the pressure of needing to feel more open to these skills than my student. Thankfully, she is a beautiful human being, and I told myself that I could trust her to know the real me — the tortured yoga teacher with a blocked third eye.

We began our first exercise as partners. Using yogic breathing, I slowed my mind down and calmed myself enough to shoot off the first thing that came to me, and I just said it. At the time, I thought I was making it up, as I have a powerful imagination. But then she validated what I told her, and in a really big way.

I could hardly believe it. I had not made it up. This was an actual intuitive knowing! This small victory sparked a new wave for me. I realized how much I had allowed my mind to hold me back. I understood that the key to my opened third eye was to not give myself any time to think. From this point on, I got good at not thinking when I needed to turn off that part of the brain. Instead, I just allowed myself to be guided by my Highest Self, which comes from the first thought or vision in a mindset that is calm and open.

These days, I flirt between different "Claire's," — the intuitive or psychic "abilities" such as clairsentience, the ability to sense emotional or psychic energy, clairaudience the ability to hear non-audible messages from spirit or higher beings, clairvoyance, having visions, clairalience, smelling scents without a physical source, and claircognizance, the clear knowing about something that is going to happen. I must say that, to date, I have not had any clairgustance occurrences. This is when one tastes food without having physically injected it. And I want to go on record as saying that I am okay with that. So if any of the Clair-gods are listening, you can keep that one. Thanks.

When I am tuned in, sometimes I smell something. Other times, I have a vision. But for me, the one that comes the most is that knowing. I've cultivated a very open portal for what many may refer to as channeling. I acknowledge many light beings, Archangels, and Ascended Masters, and I invite them to work through me.

Sometimes I know who it is, and other times I don't; I just know. For the *Game of Thrones* fans: "I meditate, and I know things."

However it comes, I do not discount what comes in. I just witness it. So when I tell a client in a Quantum Healing session that they were a mermaid in a past life on Atlantis, or that the African Mothers want me to dance to tribal music around the table, please know that I am not making this shit up. But it took me close to twenty years of cultivating ways to get here.

In my years of yoga and other ascension energy practices, I've also discovered ways to focus on what I consider to be extremely important complementary embodiment energies. While many are fans of being hyper-focused on opening the upper chakra energies, I've always admired the descending energy and the many earthly, lower chakras that critically need attention for physical manifestation. There are times when intuitive and psychic abilities come in handy or can benefit one's healing. But do not discount the significance of feeling into your being what is real.

So what is this elusive third eye? How do we open it or see out of it? And why is this important for a yogi? Or is it?

The third eye is referred to by yogis as the *Ajna chakra*, or sixth *chakra*. It is located around the center of the forehead, just above the eyes, and is considered to be related to the pineal gland. First, let's discuss the *chakra* - pronounced CHaa-kruh - remember. Mispronunciation of this word is a major peeve of mine and thus needs repeating (see page 17).

Many yogic texts discuss the *chakra* system, located within the subtle energy body. To understand the *chakras*, one needs to understand the anatomy behind them. Similar to our nervous system, there are energy lines in the body that have been outlined by the ancient yogis as *nadis*. These lines carry *pranic* energy throughout the being, which includes areas outside of the physical body.

Along the *nadis,* we encounter vortexes of energy where several *nadis* have come together, creating a vast gathering point of *prana*. These are considered to be the *chakras*.

The actual number of *chakras* is also a bit controversial. Dissimilar to our lungs, we cannot dissect the body and see the organs. Instead, you have to rely on heightened states of consciousness or technologies like aura photography — something beyond the everyday abilities of most people — to see or feel the *chakras*.

Being left to rely on these circumstances, many have chosen not to believe in the existence of these energy centers, which would be an easy thing to do, except for the fact that there's a lot that makes sense about them. I also have lots of friends who love and practice yoga based around the *chakras*, yet they couldn't tell you by any personal experience that they have seen them. And yet, those aesthetics who practiced yoga thousands of years ago saw them, felt them, and understood them enough to write about them.

From the *Hamsa Upanishad*, fourth verse:
> "...having reached *Ajna*, one contemplates in *Brahmarandhra* (in the head) and having meditated there always 'I am of three *Matras*', cognizes (his Self) and becomes formless."

This verse was written around the 17th century. I still have no idea what it means. It felt important to quote something here. And it does validate from a long time ago the third eye's significance. The *chakras* are also discussed in the famous *Rig Veda*, famous because it is mankind's oldest written knowledge, dating back to approximately 1700 BCE, yup, way older than the Bible. I know I've mentioned some of this before, but bear with me; I'm menopausal. Did I already mention that, too?

It's Okay; Odin and Frigga (his wife, she deserves a little more education as the goddess of wisdom and foresight, perhaps more than Odin in this chapter) both love us.

Remember that yoga is much older than their texts, such as the *Vedas* and *Upanishads*, as it was originally an oral tradition. But at least those who need something concrete can know that the *Chakra* system was written about over 3,000 years ago. The ancient yogis understood them to be true, and so a yoga teacher or student of the same lineage, we, therefore, trust that they are.

The number of *chakras* can be debated, but for our purposes of work here, we go by the more recent standardized number of seven major *chakras* in the human body.

The first *chakra, Muladhara,* is located at the base of the spine. It assists us in grounding our body into the earth, establishing our foundational support here.

The second *chakra, Svadhisthana,* is located in the sacral area and is said to house our emotions and assist us in accepting that joy and pleasure are divine human rights to acknowledge.

The third *chakra, Manipura,* located at the solar plexus, is our inner fire where our ego lives and breathes. It's here that we find the courage and inner strength within us to step forth in our personal power.

At the center is the heart *chakra*, *Anahata*, the ooey-gooey, love-based energy center that allows us to feel, give, and receive love unconditionally. It is a place of balance and compassion for all beings.

Above the heart is the throat *chakra*, *Vishudda*, the location of our communication area. At the fifth *chakra*, we now communicate who we are and what our truth is and also make space to listen to others. This center double identifies as also a detoxification and purification point, thereby allowing the filtering of bullshit to be released. Because, guess what? If you can't filter out the bullshit, then you cannot realize the energy of the next chakra, *Ajna*, the third-eye center. If this *chakra* cannot open, then you will not realize liberation at the crown *chakra*, where true wisdom and understanding thrive.

And that is quite literally the briefest explanation of the *chakra* system that I have ever written. Seriously, I created a full 100-hour teacher training program based around these energy vortexes, and it was a very popular program. Hundreds of hours of training and lifework condensed for you here in about the span of one page of text. Oh, the things I do for you. You're welcome.

Energy is said to flow upward from the base to the crown, in a movement towards expansion and liberation. But there is also a second current that descends from the crown to the base, allowing us to manifest into human form and consciousness. As you can suspect, the two currents merge at each *chakra* in what is referred to as a dance.

There is a lovely story about Lord *Shiva*, Master Yogi, seated on his throne at the crown *chakra*, lost in Meditation. Meanwhile, his wife, *Parvati*, in the form of *Shakti*, or Divine Creation, dances her way upward from the sacral *chakra*. Her intoxicating dance is said to awaken the yogi, and he makes his descent downward. Eventually, the two lovers meet at the heart. Many people encounter this sweet love story and are moved to tears. It is very cute. But all I see is the woman, once again, doing all the work, being the true master. But I digress.

It is easy to see the significance that the yogi puts on opening the third eye. This area is responsible for pre-cognition, intuition, visions, illuminations, astral travels, and clairvoyance. It is the step before full knowledge and understanding that comes from a lifetime of practice and devotion to yoga. While the other *chakras* are aligned quite a bit to our physicality, at the *Ajna chakra,* we seem to move to another level, beyond the body and mind, to an arena that we romanticize as the epitome of an awakened state of consciousness.

The emphasis on this chakra has supported many aspiring yogis to work tirelessly in the upward current, therefore becoming trapped in the upper energy centers while seemingly floating through life without substantial grounding and foundational support that assists in one successfully surviving life on planet Earth. Many have devoted their lives to ascending out of the body, beyond the earth, and into the heavenly realms.

To everyone, may I remind you, again, that you took human form for a reason. Your purpose on earth is not to ascend and leave your body. One is too centered in one's ego if one believes so. Your purpose is to merge your inner earth and star on planet Earth, in the heart, birthing a New Reality of Oneness right here, collectively.

If you are a true yogi, you stay centered in your heart, working tirelessly for the betterment of all life. I'm sorry to burst your bubble if you were ready to leave us all behind in your quest to master yoga or the misunderstood idea of ascension.

To me, it is more important to keep the heart open and stay centered there than to worry about whether your third eye is open, closed, or blocked. If you stay at the heart and allow energy to flow in both directions from there, eventually, things will balance out. Your intuition will enhance, your body will become stronger yet more flexible, and you will continue to unlock more abilities.

Go ahead and admit when energy is blocked or closed. It doesn't make you a bad yogi. Frankly, it may make you a better one. And if things start to open a crack, and a little black bird flies into your third eye, take it as a positive omen.

Raven or not, the All-Father, Odin, and his two ravens, Huginn (meaning thought) and Muninn (meaning memory or mind), most certainly love you. Invite them in!

CHAPTER 7

THAT'S NEVER GOING TO HAPPEN, I'M BEING REALISTIC

*"If at first you don't succeed,
then skydiving definitely isn't for you."*
~ Steven Wright

The year was 2019, and I had just concluded a successful retreat in Thailand. A good friend and I celebrated by heading south to tour the Thai Islands. Our first stop was Krabi, where a famous Buddha sits atop Tiger Cave Temple, approximately 309 meters vertically, along a 600-meter path comprised of 1260 steps. Easy-peasy!

The nice gentleman who drove us to the temple had lived in Krabi his entire life and never attempted the climb. He told us that most Thai people do not. In his exact words, "It's for the tourists." Okay, but I still wanted to do it.

My friend and I began our trek up the vertical climb, and about fifty steps in, I told her not to wait for me. So she proceeded upward, and I sat down for a moment to reflect on my choices.

Already, the view was spectacular. I could only imagine the spectacular view at the pinnacle, and I looked forward to seeing that and the large golden Buddha seated at the top. I would attempt another 20 or maybe 30 steps and take another pause. In the beginning stages, the thing about the climb that assisted me in continuing was the fabulous people headed down, encouraging me to continue up.

At one point, I met a group of girls who were too scared to climb up past the pack of aggressive monkeys known for stealing sunglasses, water bottles, snacks, and any other items you dared reveal to them. I wasn't scared of the monkeys, but I also wasn't sure I could make it to the top. So, together we encouraged each other to keep going, which was nice for a while — until I got them past the monkeys, and then they left me.

I continued inching upward, slowly, stopping frequently to evaluate what the fuck I was doing it all for.

At one point, I stopped encouraging myself to keep going and started cursing a whole lot, telling myself, "You can't do this. You are not going to make it to the top. It's okay to stop and go down. You will never make it. You can't do it." I would get so pissed off at myself, I would get up and walk another 20 or 30 steps or so, and drop back down into a wailing heap of negativity. But that negative banter moved me forward when the positive talk no longer worked. I simply gave in and honored those feelings, and it worked for me, propelling me upwards.

I eventually did make it to the top and took some fabulous pictures once there, dedicating the climb to my Grandmother, Rachel, who had recently passed away, never having the opportunity to climb much since she was born with polio, which restricted some of her physical abilities. But that never stopped her from believing in herself. If she was told that she could not attain something, she did it just to prove doctors and other people wrong. I never knew a stronger-willed woman than her, and after a strenuous climb, I could think of no other person but her. She would have been proud of me. She would have thought I was nuts like the Krabi driver but would have been proud, nonetheless.

The point is, I'd done it. I had made it to the top. I hated every moment of that climb, though. And I made a vow to never find myself needing to tackle it ever again. That evening, I had one of the best Thai massages. I even fell asleep during it. That massage alone was worth the climb! No, it wasn't. Maybe? I'm still mulling that all over. However, I can state with complete certainty that given the opportunity again, or even one similar, I will take the Thai massage and skip the climb. Knowing I can, and did, is enough.

When it comes to possibilities, I have always been one who is convinced that anything is possible. I believe in magic and that we are magical beings capable of anything we truly put our hearts and souls into. This does not mean that I am always successful at everything that I put myself to, yet I still hold space for all the possibilities. In fact, in recent years, I have come to make space for even more than what I can quantify in my limited perception as being possible.

So what is possible? What are the limits of possibility? How do we quantify these to determine the probability of any particular thing happening?

First, let's tackle the concept of what is possible. Well, that line of questioning does not get me far because I have to stop and consider the person. What is possible for one person is surely not for another.

Real-life case:
Due to a cervical spine issue, I never pushed myself to practice advanced inversions and kept to the modifications. However, each time I watch someone pop up into a Handstand, it looks so effortless that I believe I can pop right into it myself. Since I teach people how to perform the posture with much success, I figured one day I would be ready, willing, and able to come into the pose.

With a polished, positive attitude, I stepped next to the wall, kicked up my legs, and realized I had only lifted a few inches off the floor. I think one would be hard-pressed to consider what I did even an inversion. But, as the great hockey player Wayne Gretzky was known to say, "You miss one hundred percent of the shots you never take." And since transference doesn't apply to many things, you just have to take the shot, practice, and work on stuff to master most of them.

The three P's of practice, patience, and perseverance are usually necessary when tackling most things. And that's where the yoga practice applies well.

The ancient yogis talked about what are referred to as paranormal abilities. Known as the *siddhis*, these accomplishments are considered to be the consequence of an austere spiritual practice. For the novice practitioner and those at the local yoga *shala*, yoga scripture says that you may get a glimpse at one or two of these but will not see them all to fruition. But since I like to believe that anything is possible, perhaps we have given too much weight to the aesthetics and their method of practicing. What if householders can also reach the same place with the right intention?

In my older age, I am leaning towards feeling that the yogic rhetoric was meant to keep us in check, to keep the householders held back so that we don't realize our full potential.

There was also a time, not so long ago, when women were told that they could not practice yoga. Today, women account for more than 74% of the practitioners in the world, according to a blog from the National Yoga Alliance in November 2023[8]. My grandmother would have been an amazing yogi. She already had the focus of one.

Since women are reclaiming much of their power in the world today, I'll put my money on us figuring out these *siddhis* too. So for all the women out there, working full time, running their households like a Fortune-500 business, nurturing their families, and still finding time for their self-care, let's pour over these magical abilities, and figure them the fuck out.

There are eight main *siddhis* in Vedic literature:
- *Anima* = reducing the body to the size of an atom
- *Mahima* = expanding the body infinitely larger

---

[8] https://blog.yogaalliance.org/2023/11/15/press-release-yoga-in-the-world-research-study/#:~:text=71%20percent%20of%20yoga%20practitioners,versus%2042.8%20percent%2C%20respectively).

- *Garima* = becoming infinitely heavy
- *Laghima* = become weightless
- *Prapti* = having unrestricted access to all places
- *Prakamya* = the ability to materialize anything at will
- *Ishitva* = possessing the ability to create, sustain, and destroy all matter at will
- *Vasitva* = the ability to control all material elements or natural forces

My first thoughts when reading about these *siddhis* were of *Alice in Wonderland*. Through the eyes of the imagination of Lewis Carroll, we certainly entertain the possibilities that abound for the human being, even if it be in an alternate universe. But the musings of fiction often are derived from the truths in life they are fond of saying, which is stranger than the conjured option. That's a fancy way of saying, "Truth is stranger than fiction." I was trying to be more of a wordsmith.

While these eight *siddhis* are said to be the primary ones, *Patanjali* lists over twenty other *siddhis* for us in his *Yoga Sutras*. Some of these include invisibility, remote vision, mind reading, levitation, influencing others, and more.

Now, we are starting to sound more like a Marvel comic superhero. Can you imagine a superhero called simply "The Yogi?" He materializes out of nowhere, levitates, and reveals that he not only knows that you cheated on your vegan diet but that he saw you cook and eat bacon-wrapped scallops last weekend. There's no hiding from The Yogi! Watch out, criminals, you know who you are, those that steal famous quotes as your own and walk out of the yoga *shala* with their props. The Yogi knows which yoga studio you're planning to use your Groupon at next and will thwart your every attempt. You know, that's a pretty badass superhero. And since I already own the uniform, I guess I just need to figure out these elusive *siddhis*!

Ah, but if the *siddhis* are supposed to be available to any yogi, do we have any direct recognition of anyone achieving these accomplishments?

In the yoga tradition, another book that has been given the title of "One of the 100 Best Spiritual Books of the Twentieth Century," *Autobiography of a Yogi*, written by Paramahansa Yogananda, tells the story of his life as he searched throughout India for a spiritual teacher. He conveys the personal accounts of witnessing sages and saints attain *siddhis* throughout the book, which is said to be one of the classics in spiritual literature.

When I first read *Autobiography of a Yogi*, it reaffirmed my feelings about human capabilities. The extraordinary has always fascinated and captivated me. As a young child, when asked what I wanted to be when I grew up, I said, "A Magician!" Not the "pull a rabbit out of my hat" one, though. The allure of that title for my young self was that it was the closest thing to realizing the unlimited human possibilities that I had heard put into words. It was about real magic.

For a child, anything is possible. But as adults, we are often told that we have to be more realistic. I'm vastly entertained by the establishments that push this agenda down our throats as the go-to reality. Why, as children, is it okay to imagine, play, and entertain unlimited possibilities, but not as an adult?

Somewhere, we learned that being an adult meant being more responsible and that in this element, certain things had to be put aside. But I challenge the thought that responsibility has anything to do with being realistic.

I believe quite the opposite: that being a very responsible person means questioning those who want to limit you and opening yourself up to many other levels of reality. I believe this is the key that the awakened yogis understood quite well. And I believe that we can attain the written *siddhis* and more if we open ourselves up to a worldview with more childlike wonderment.

There is a state that yogis call *samadhi,* and it is said to be the culmination of the yogi's practice. *Samadhi* is a place where individual and universal consciousness unifies, creating a space of complete calm, connection to all, and transcendence of the ordinary. For thousands and thousands of years (remember, we are still debating how old yoga is), yogis have gone to great lengths to achieve this state of *samadhi.*

Many practitioners today claim that they have achieved it, sometimes during yoga practice and other times elsewhere. Every yoga school talks about it, and yogis everywhere rejoice when they glimpse it, only to realize that the state is as fleeting as an orgasm. Of course, only a *Tantric* practitioner would know. Please refer back to Chapter 1 in the event you have forgotten this valuable lesson. However, I'm not writing the *Mahabharata* here, so you should recall.

According to our *Yoga Sutras,* the *siddhis* are attained by the yogi who can sustain *dharana* or concentration, *dhyana* or meditation, and *samadhi* at will. Thus, the reason why so many yogis focus on that upward current of awakening the third eye, yet fail to realize that this is still an embodiment practice. Again, please pay attention, and for those of you with short-term memory, refer back to Chapter 6.

So, here you are, the loyal yogi, committed to your practice, working on merging mind, body, and soul with universal consciousness every single beautiful fucking day, and your reward is becoming infinitely heavy…Wait, what? I mean, I'm pretty sure I can do that simply by eating at Mickey D's every day and supersizing. But that's not the point. And I have a great story for the point, so you'll have to hang in just a little longer.

One time (if you are a Gen Xer, you are now required to say, "At band camp," and if you are not, go ask your mom or grandma what this means) when I was home, I started to feel quite sick. My husband had already left for work, which was an hour away, but a good friend who lived with us at the time was still home. I told her that I thought I needed to go to the hospital, but as she had to leave for work soon, she called my husband. He was convinced that the pain and vomiting I was experiencing was just something that I had eaten and that it needed to pass through me.

Later that day, as my appendix was bursting, (note: that was the last time I listened to my husband about my health and well-being. And, fun fact, some years later, he would also not listen to this same advice of his and also winded up with an emergency appendectomy while I was in Greece hosting a yoga retreat. Did we discuss *karma* yet?), I sat in the hospital ER waiting room, rocking myself back and forth, spontaneously performing *ujjayi* breathing.

I found myself suspended in time, both in my body and outside of my body — expansive yet incredibly small. I felt myself move through and beyond the pain to a place where I no longer felt the physical suffering. Hovering, timeless, I possessed access to another dimension and traveled there willingly until the time when I felt my girlfriend nudging me back to be moved into a private room.

When I opened my eyes, she looked at me and said, "Dude, where did you go?" Some time, perhaps an hour or more, had passed, yet I felt no pain and had no sense of time or space. The place I went to was full of love and comfort. Although I could not see anything, I felt a deep sense of peace and connection to a bigger energy beyond my physical self — a place that had my friend not nudged me back from, I would have gladly stayed.

This was the first time I successfully achieved *samadhi* through *dharana* and *dhyana*. It is difficult for me to separate the states, as they seemed to occur simultaneously for me, as is what most yogic texts seem to confirm. At the time of my achieving *samadhi* in the ER, I had a fairly strong yoga *asana* and pranayama practice. I taught about six yoga classes a week plus ran two simultaneous yoga teacher training courses, which ran most weekends. So I taught 6-7 days a week. Yoga was a huge part of my life. You know what else was a big part of my life at this time? Homemade kombucha tea, which I am positive contributed to, if not completely inspired, the ruptured appendix.

I also had a large home an hour away from the studio, so I could easily be found cursing at other cars on the NJ Turnpike for two hours a day. Our many weekly social engagements often included party food for dinner and alcoholic spirits instead of water. Making time for my meditation practice was not even a thought, although I did have a strong earth-based spiritual practice that I tended to daily.

It's easy to see that although I ran a successful yoga studio, I would not say that I would not have been defined as a great yogi by any traditional means. Therefore, my ER achievement hadn't come from austere yoga practice with sensory withdrawal.

So, if *samadhi* is possible, why not the *siddhis*? And if the *siddhis* are possible, isn't anything and everything else?

"That's not going to happen, I'm being realistic."
Is this quote something a yogi shouldn't say? Of course, it is. Any practitioner of yoga gets the sense of wonderment and wildly magical elements of the practice, although, to *Patanjali* and other authors of the texts, these are not magical but rather ordinary states of being that the yogi can achieve.

It is true then: never say never, eat junk food to attain the yogic superpowers, and always remember, Hecate loves you — in all of her forms, Maiden, Mother, and Crone, she loves you. And she knows a thing or two about magic.

Do you know who else worked magic? Jesus. You know, he was a super yogi himself. Word has it that he cursed a lot. Well, that depends on which book you read. Or maybe it wasn't in any books. Perhaps that's because they were burned in the fire of the Library of Alexandria. Or maybe they're all hidden in the Vatican vault. Uh-oh, did I say that? Yes, I did.

Listen, my point is that you are loved.

Just be the best you can be and love others as much as you can. And if you practice yoga, then keep practicing. And if you don't practice yoga but bought the book because of the curse word on the title, maybe you want to give it a shot too — especially since you know now that yogis are everyday folks like you and I, who make mistakes and have plenty of challenges, but in the end, are motivated by our True and Highest Self to navigate through life with purpose.

And there's still more…

CHAPTER 8

I AM MY OWN GURU

"There are so many things that pop up. If you are paying attention, you can learn every second of the day. Life is my guru."
~ Jeff Bridges

In the yoga lineages, the *guru*, or spiritual guide and teacher, historically plays a significant role for the disciple. Before there were yoga studios, gyms, retreat centers, and at-home Peloton systems to practice in, a student went to live with his teacher to learn the practices of *yoga*. What you learned back then came from your teacher, specifically tailored for you, not in a cookie-cutter fashion of 26 postures performed precisely in one way. Your teacher decided when you were ready to advance to other aspects of the practice. There was no internet to watch Sally Sweetheart's Sweaty Arm Balancing Flow or to learn more postures because you were bored with the ones taught at the yoga *shala*.

For these yogis, the focus on philosophies and ways of living became more significant than even the postures and breathing techniques in understanding the yogic life, unlike today when fitting yoga into your busy schedule is somewhat difficult to manage, so you opt for the mocha latte grande and a stop at your favorite bohemian shop for some retail therapy instead. It's okay if you do; Hathor loves you.

When I first opened my yoga studio in New Jersey, there were not many others in the area. The few studios that existed at that time did not welcome me with open arms. I heard whispers of some harsh words that they had to say about me:

"Who is she to have a yoga studio?"

"What makes her think she can teach yoga?"

"She doesn't even have a yoga lineage!"

Oh, and there were more. I worked very hard to prove to myself and to the greater community that I was able to teach and train others in the practice of yoga. There were notable times at local yoga events when I was slighted by other studio owners and teachers. I had this naive vision back then that all yoga studios could work together to create a big community and all thrive together. The judgments and the lack of love for me and about me was astonishing. I wondered how they could call themselves yoga studios with these mindsets. The hypocrisy was, frankly, astonishing.

One fine day, another one of the other local studio owners in the Princeton area called me up to welcome me and invite me to an event with the well-known teacher Dharma Mittra. I thought to myself, here we go, now I have to defend myself again. But actually, he was quite lovely. He asked me frankly who my *guru* was. Without hesitation, I shot straight back to him, "I don't have one."

I braced myself for the backlash, and then he kindly replied, "That's okay, you don't need one."

I was rendered speechless. This was the first random act of kindness I had received from another studio owner since I opened mine. While it took me a moment to regain my footing, he shared the story of his *guru* and how that came about for him. Then, our conversation concluded with an invitation to the event, which I gratefully attended.

For some time, I pondered the need or relevance of a *guru*. Every time I went to see *kirtan* artist Krishna Das, the devotion to his *guru* rang through as such deep truth that I longed for one myself.

My first yoga teacher closed her studio and left the area quite soon after I graduated from my yoga teacher training program with her. In her wake, she left no invitation to reconnect. From the beginning of my journey as a yoga teacher, I felt adrift, alone, figuring it out as I went along, hoping that I was making a difference for my students and learning from the many mistakes that I made along the way.

The closest I came to having a *guru* was when I met Amma, known at that time as the "Hugging Mother." She came through the Princeton area on a tour one summer, and I had this feeling that I needed to see her. So, I went to the temple and waited my turn to have a private moment with her. At the time, I was dealing with a lot of sadness and loss in my life. My heart was very heavy, and even though I knew why, I didn't know what to do about it or how to change it. A deep, overwhelming sadness followed me everywhere I went. Most people did not notice, except the few who were very close to me. I was good at hiding shit back then.

When it was my turn, I walked up to Amma and gazed into her eyes. I could feel such a level of truth, love, and compassion. What she said to me proved immediately that she could see my grief — she could see all of me — and almost immediately, I began to weep.

In her presence, I understood the intoxication that people feel when with their *gurus*. And I recognized why I might want to feel seen at such a profound level as this daily. Yet I also knew that I needn't rely on another so completely because that was outward seeking. And if I was truly to find wholeness again within my being, then I couldn't seek it through someone else.

But I did not always feel this way.

As a young girl, I was quite timid. As I became a young woman, I was wrought with a lack of courage and self-worth. I grew up believing that I always needed someone, a teacher or a partner, to assist me in life. I believe that the Universe always puts us in positions that we need, providing us with constant situations in which to learn from, grow, and enhance ourselves.

So the Universe continually put me in situations where I needed to learn how to stand on my own, find inner strength, and lean on her. It continues to offer me these opportunities every time I start to slack in this area. Is it with great love and perfect surrender that I align with these challenges? No, I fight it, just like you do. I fight it, I whine and cry, I make excuses, I pity myself, and then in the end, I accept it. Because it's the only other thing to do. But not without a whole lot of immaturity. I'm still learning, and that's why I still get the lessons. Thanks?

I credit my yoga practice with providing me with a proven method to find my inner strength. But in truth, I also had strong examples in my life to model for me.

I would be remiss if I didn't mention another touchy subject for yogis regarding *gurus*: misconduct and abuse.

Oy, this is a big one. Where do I begin?

I became aware of this issue from my first yoga teacher, who had recommended Steven Cope's book, *Yoga and the Quest for the True Self*. It's an amazing book that I highly recommend. Cope was a psychologist and yoga practitioner who took a sabbatical and went to Kripalu Center for Yoga and Health in Stockbridge, Massachusetts, to immerse himself in an *ashram* setting and study under the tutelage of Swami Kripalu's disciple, Amrit Desai, the self-professed *guru* of Kripalu. In 1994, leaks about Desai's involvement in sexual abuse with several female *ashram* residents while in this role surfaced, even though he touted staunch celibacy for himself and all practicing yogis.

The stories of Desai's charismatic presence are widely known. This quality seems to be a recurring one when various *gurus* are mentioned. I've heard yogis say that when their *guru* gazed upon them, it was as if the eyes of God were looking back at them.

This is a tricky subject. People have differing belief systems about God. Some consider God to be a separate entity, while others, like our yogis, believe that God, or divine essence, resides within. I can see why some would be confused. Perhaps it's one of those "What came first, the Chicken or the Egg?" things. This goes back to that question of us being either a human being having a spiritual experience or a spiritual being having a human experience.

Therefore, there's a confusion with the sentiment of the *guru's* eyes being God looking back. Since we cannot come to a solid agreement on this, we have to stick with what we do know: man is human. It's right there in the word: hu-MAN. And so it is, for sure, the eyes of a human being. And when a human being is elevated to the level of a quasi-god, that ever-pervading ego emerges. Remember that? (Chapter 4).

The fact is that over the years, the number of cases of sexual misconduct with yoga teachers elevated to *guru* status is staggering. The most well-known may now be Bikram Choudhury, who somehow copyrighted his sequence and style of yoga. When a court ruled in his favor over that copyright, I nearly lost it. We don't even know the precise age of this practice because it's so old. But somehow, several thousands of years later, in the late 1900s, one dude in California managed to claim a portion of it as his. Unbelievable!

P.S. Bikram is the predecessor of Hot Yoga, so if that's your style, he's your Grandpa. And it appears that Grandpa was a very dirty boy. From allegations of sexual assault and rape to other abuses and discrimination, Bikram was forced to flee the USA in 2016 after an arrest warrant was issued for him for not paying over 6 million in damages. There's a documentary if you'd like to learn more about him and the horrendous acts and allegations. But, unfortunately, he's not the only one.

In 2012, *Anusara* founder John Friend was accused of being in a Wiccan Coven and having sex with several of the married female coven members. This and other allegations of a fiduciary nature led to Friend leaving *Anusara* and the entire empire crumbling virtually overnight. I recall it vividly.

At the time, *Anusara* Yoga was the hot new style of *Hatha* Yoga in town. All the cool kids were doing it and learning to teach it. Having learned himself from people like Swami Satchidananda, Integral Yoga founder, and B.K.S. Iyengar, founder of Iyengar Yoga, I found Friend's *Anusara* to be nothing more than a blend of those and other styles of *Hatha* Yoga wrapped up in a pretty bow — his charismatic nature. Friend's exploits mimicked Desai's, and when I tell you that literally overnight, nobody even wanted to breathe the word *Anusara*, I am not kidding. One day, it was just done, and nobody wanted to even talk about it or admit to being a part of it.

Speaking of Swami Satchidananda, yes, eventually, even allegations about this great *guru* surfaced. You may have heard of him as the "Woodstock *Guru*," as he was the man who opened up Woodstock in 1969 with an opening prayer of peace and love. He not only founded a style of *Hatha* Yoga but also opened the famous Yogaville in Buckingham County, Virginia. This headquarters *ashram* boasts the famous LOTUS shrine, dedicated to the unity of world religions, and cost $2 million to construct. It's a beautiful place where I spent hours contemplating how world religions are more similar than different. Swami Satchidananda co-founded my seminary school, the first Interfaith Seminary in the world, The New Seminary, along with Rabbi Joseph Gelberman and the Very Rev. James P. Morton, a Catholic Priest. I know, every time I hear that, I also hear it as a joke: "So, a Rabbi, Catholic Priest, and *Guru* walk into a bar…"

Swami Satchidananda wrote many books under the Integral Yoga umbrella. I used many of these in my yoga teacher training programs. He was beloved and did so much to further the causes of yoga and Interfaith religious efforts in the world. He was even given a peace prize. But guess what? In 1991, several former disciples accused him of sexual misconduct with them. Swami Satchidananda denied the claims, but several board members stepped down, and a support group was founded to assist the victims. You decide.

I could continue the list of *gurus* with shady pasts, but you get the gist. It's a sad commentary about a practice that can catapult one into the realms of pure bliss and knowing the True Self. But there's that idea of leaning into something — someone — outside of one's self for validation that, in my humble opinion, is the root problem of it all.

During a panel discussion regarding my Doctoral Thesis in my Interfaith Ministerial program, a panelist asked me to define my religious beliefs. I explained how my parents permitted me to figure out my own beliefs. Having the freedom to discover what I believed led me down a long path of discovering what was true for me, and that was a belief in my Highest Self and an alignment with the divinity within me. This led back to a discussion about my Grandmother, Rachel, who, although born with polio, spent her life in defiance of that limitation, proving to the world that she was unstoppable.

After I shared my belief system at the panel discussion, I was sure that my conditional Doctorate was about to be revoked. But the opposite happened. This same panelist expressed his impression that finding God within us was most likely the highest form of spiritual aspiration one could attain. And then, just like that, I became a Doctor of Ministry. And it was not because of my devout love for Jesus or Lao Tzu, Isis or Buddha (although I do love them all), but because of my devout love of my True Self, the part of us that is timeless and, at its essence, always present and in alignment in Oneness.

To circle back, don't think the irony isn't lost on me about my belief in divine essence within. However, I don't consider myself a *guru*, and dislike it whenever a former student calls me one, even jokingly. Or do I? Well, the human side of me does kind of like it. Ego again. See, can't get away from it. Yet where there's ego, there's also humility.

Several years into teaching, I realized while instructing a yoga class that some of my students had surpassed my abilities on the mat. They required more from their *asana* practice than what I was giving them. So, I began teaching more advanced postures to give them something to "work on" that challenged them. I taught this way for a few years until I had a true epiphany. It wasn't the postures so much that mattered. What I needed to stretch was their perceptions and mental limitations. This gave rise to deeply themed practices whereby I dropped in nuggets of yogic and other spiritual philosophies for them to marinate over while holding the postures that applied to that relevant theme.

This change in my teaching style corresponded with a shift in my student base. Those who were not ready to find their truth and sought yoga more as a physical practice or workout started to move on to other studios with fast-paced flows and action-packed practices. The students that started to come to me were real people, and often broken — yes, sometimes with physical limitations, but also with broken hearts, minds, and souls. Yoga became their sanctuary, their church, their place to feel and heal.

I held this sacred space for hundreds of students over the years. And I can fondly recall many who allowed the practice in and to create a level of understanding of their True Self, transforming off the mat and creating a life more aligned to that trueness.

During an immersive 500-hour training, a teacher trainee came to a deep truth in her life and made a very difficult decision that would impact every aspect of her life. At first, I was worried that I had encouraged her to make choices that gave way to too much difficulty. But I soon came to realize that her inner *guru* was guiding her, not me. Her truth was so significant that she had no choice but to make this decision. It took a few years for her to move through this challenging period of her life before landing in such a beautiful place that she would have never known had she not made that initial, tough decision. Her inner *guru* had led her to true happiness.

By listening to their inner *gurus,* I've watched many of my students move out of their comfort zones to find joy and peace in their lives. I like to think that some of my teachings assisted them in these realizations. But I never told them what they should do. Instead, I listened, I held a sacred space for them, and I stretched them where they needed it.

The reciprocity I received from my students was truly a gift, for they have been my true teachers. In my twenty-two years of owning a yoga studio, I learned more from my students than I believe I ever could have through one single teacher. It was through them that I learned how to be a good yoga teacher, an honest friend, and a beloved human being, sometimes even by making mistakes. And it was through them that I finally allowed myself to listen to my own inner *guru*.

It started when I heard many of my students repeat my teachings back to me and share how I had helped them in their lives. It continued when I went against my intuition and mishandled a relationship or situation and lost a student and friend. It reveals itself to me continually when a former student reaches out to me and shares a part of their life and how yoga has helped them get through the tough times.

Ram Das, the spiritual teacher, said, "I hang out with my *guru* in my heart. And I love everything in the universe."

I love this quote as it relays the message that you need to stay focused in your heart to connect to anything seemingly outward. By going within and holding a loving space, we find what we truly seek. Now that's juicy stuff.

Several years ago, many in the various new age communities began to state that "the age of the *guru* is over." In awakening to the new energies on earth, there was an urgency to relate this to folks. Yet, I see it as something a little different.

Since we have been on earth, we have been living under the constructs of a reality system of "Duality." In this system, we have learned that things are either male or female, good or bad, spiritual or not spiritual. Everything that has been built in this system is built on the foundation of duality. Now we find ourselves on the precipice of birthing a New Reality: Oneness. In this reality system, all things birthed in duality can no longer exist. This includes spiritual practices aligned as such.

One of the things I have always enjoyed about yoga is the fact that it is timeless. It is a true system whereby the individual can work to move into Oneness. If I am aligned in Oneness, then all the answers that I seek are within. A good teacher can lead you down the path, but it is only you who can walk through the door and claim this.

Maybe in the past, when I was lost in duality, lost in systems that did not always have my best interests in mind, lost in constructs where man somehow managed to misconstrue the truths, maybe then I needed or thought that I needed the help of a spiritual *guru*. But now that I am aligned on the path of the Oneness, I understand that I only need to go inside my own heart to find my way.

We will always have challenges to move through in life while we are in human form. Not everything is cupcakes and puppies (or rainbows and unicorns, add in your favorite things). Having other like-minded, loving souls to assist you through these ups and downs is surely going to be helpful and important.

Will you learn from them?

You betcha!

Will they be your teachers?

Yup.

But will you need a *guru* to lean on?

Most likely not. Not for those who are awakened on the path of love.

For those of you with a *guru*, please understand that this may be a way for you to continue to connect with what works for you. I certainly understand the energy transference you receive from this spiritual being. But never discount your own inner *guru*, for she is the one who will be with you through it all and to the end.

And remember, She loves you.

EPILOGUE

Well, we did it together. You made it to the end of my book. Yay for us! I attempted to touch upon most of the significant aspects of yoga and provide you with both personal information and researched knowledge. I hope that I made good arguments for the chapter titles as I discussed topics that yogis should or shouldn't say.

These are all part and parcel of my observations in my twenty-five years of teaching yoga, nearly thirty years of personal practice, and over 22,000 teaching hours. Funny, I remember when the National Yoga Alliance began, and they created their foundations for being a yoga teacher versus an "Experienced" Yoga teacher. Today, they have broken the "Experienced" thing down into various hours. The highest tier is an Experienced 1500-hour Yoga Teacher, which requires you to have taught 6000 hours. You do the math. It's okay, I did it for you: I'm almost the highest-tiered type of teacher four times over. I'm not bragging. I'm simply stating a quantifiable way to support the fact that I know some shit about yoga.

So, if you want to argue about any of the points that I have made in the book, I suggest this: write your own damn book.

And if you feel that I've offended you in any of my chapters, let me just call bullshit one more time. I do not have the power to offend anyone. You can be offended, but that's entirely your shit. Own it.

I've always said that the best teachers are mirrors. If you don't like what you see in it, change it. But it starts with you. Many of my former teacher trainees have said over the years that I am a "hard teacher." I hope they meant difficult. I'd hate to be confused with any misconduct of the *gurus*. Besides, I'm a girl. And to my knowledge, there's never been a female *guru* accused of such things as their male counterparts. So, I have that going for me.

What began as a cathartic method of releasing the many mixed feelings I had after closing my yoga studio has finally come to an end. I wanted to conclude by saying I love you. Despite my potty-mouth and sarcastic NJ whit, I fucking love you. Please send me some love back. Five stars on Amazon will be an awesome start. But I'm open to where this can take us.

Sincerest gratitude,

Tracey, or if you prefer, Dr. T.

GLOSSARY

Abhinivesha - the fifth klesha, referred to as the fear of death or attachment to life

Ahimsa - the first Yama, meaning non-stealing

Ajna - the sixth chakra, also called the third-eye chakra, the seat of intuition, the right to truly see

Anahata - the fourth chakra, also referred to as the heart center, is known for being the bridge between the upper and lower chakras and the embodiment of love and compassion

Anandamaya Kosha - bliss body, the final kosha/layer, representing a state of pure joy, peace, and spiritual fulfillment

Anima - the first siddhi, said to bring the yogi the power to reduce the body to the size of an atom

Anjali Mudra - a common hand gesture meaning "offering" used in yoga, commonly referred to as "prayer gesture"

Annamaya Kosha - body sheath, the first kosha/layer related to the outermost part of the human person

Anusara - style of yoga developed by John Friend in 1997, meaning "flowing with grace," blending biomechanics principles and heart-centered philosophy

Aparigraha - a Yama meaning non-possessiveness or non-attachment

Arjuna - a central figure in Hindu mythology, prominently featured in the Mahabharata and Bhagavad Gita, who is known for his piety

Asana - yogic postures for stretching and strengthening the body, literally meaning to find one's seat

Ashram - a spiritual community, typically centered around a guru

Asmita - the second klesha, over-identifying with the ego

Asteya - the third Yama, meaning non-stealing

Avidya - the first klesha, meaning ignorance

Ayurveda - a traditional Indian method of natural healing, often followed in conjunction with yoga, focusing on balancing the elemental energy in the body

Bandha - a Sanskrit word meaning lock or bind, where the yogi uses muscle groups to control the flow of energy through a valve-type mechanism

Bhagavad Gita - Hindu scripture that is part of the epic Mahabharata focusing on a moment in time where a dialogue between Arjuna and God, as his charioteer, occurs just moments before he is to go to battle against his family

Bhakti - yoga of devotion, where the human emotional force is purified and channeled towards the divine

BKS Iyengar - founder of a style of yoga called Iyengar focusing on prop use for correct alignment in postures

Brahmacharya - the fourth Yama, meaning moderation or chastity, depending on the translation

Buddha - a historical person who attained enlightenment and founded Buddhism to teach others this path

Chakra - wheel or disk, also referred to as the energy centers, which are a convergence of pranic energy in a location of the body within the main Nadi channel (Sushumna)

Clairalience - the ability to smell scents without a physical source, often tied to memories or presences

Clairaudience - the ability to hear voices, sounds, or messages not audible to the physical ears and often thought to be from spiritual sources, guides, or inner wisdom

Claircognizance - the ability to instantly gain unexplained knowledge without reasoned evidence

Clairgustance - the ability to taste something without it being in your mouth, often symbolically tied to a spiritual presence

Clairsentience - the ability to sense emotions, physical sensations, or energy, intuitively, without a direct cause

Clairvoyance - the ability to see things beyond "normal" vision like images, visions, symbols, past, present, and future

Dharma Mittra - a renowned yoga teacher in NYC known for creating the Master Yoga Chart in 1984, photographing himself in 1300 poses that were cut and pasted onto a poster pre-digital age, eventually spotlighting a sequence of 908 postures

Dharana - the sixth of Patanjali's eight limbs, meaning concentration, and is the practice of holding single-pointed focus on a single object

Dhyana - the seventh of Patanjali's eight limbs, meaning contemplation, and occurs when the focus becomes effortless without any struggle to concentrate — just pure flow of awareness

Dvesha - the fourth klesha, meaning repulsion

Eight Limbs/Eight Limbs of Yoga/Eight Limbs of Patanjali - the first written foundation codifying yoga, a classical text from Patanjali, also known as Ashtanga. These limbs are: Yama, Niyama, Asana, Pranayama, Pratyahara, Dharana, Dhyana, and Samadhi

Garima - the third siddhi, said to assist the yogi in becoming infinitely heavy

Generation X - the "best" generation, those born between 1965 and 1980, although some say 1961 - 1981, whose attitude is often pegged as cynical, independent, and skeptical of authority. Gen-X/Gen-Xers are known for drinking hose water, being gone from home all day without their parents' care or awareness of where they were, and being the only generation to become 30 when they were 13 and still be 30 at 50.

Guru - a spiritual teacher or guide, rooted in the Hindu, Buddhist, Jainism, or Sikhism traditions, coming from the Sanskrit "Gu" meaning "darkness" and "ru" meaning remover; therefore, a guru dispels darkness and is thus a bringer of light

Hamsa Upanishad - a Sanskrit text attached to the *Shukla Yajurveda*, one of the four Vedas, reflecting on mystical practices, the soul, and ultimate unity through yoga practices

Hanuman - Hindu monkey god, known for his devotion

Hatha - the "forceful yoga," or the branch of yoga focusing on the body known for postures, breathing, and cleansing practices

Ishitva - the seventh siddhi, said to allow the yogi to create, sustain, and destroy at will

Ishvara Pranidhana - the fifth Niyama, meaning to surrender to God

Jalandhara Bandha - the throat lock that is performed when the muscles of the throat are drawn backward and up, done by tucking the chin and lengthening the back of the neck upward

Janna - yoga of knowledge or wisdom, said to be the ability to discern the real from the unreal

Jesus - in the Christian tradition, the son of God, and in other traditions a prophet or teacher

Karma - yoga of action, where every action is a form of sacrifice, ultimately creating freedom of ego so that the action and being for a spontaneous feedback loop. Some people refer to this as "what goes around, comes around"

Kirtan - a call-and-response style of changing or singing of mantras, hymns, or the name of God

Klesha - the causes of suffering

Konnichiwa - hello in Japanese

Kumbukha - the retention aspect of the breath, used when performing the 4,4, 8 breathing technique

Kundalini - an enormous reservoir of untapped energy within the human person, and in this style of yoga founded by Yogi Bhajan, one can access and utilize this creative power for the evolution of consciousness

Laghima - the fourth siddhi, said to assist the yogi in becoming weightless

Ma Durga - Hindu Goddess revered in all of her forms and known as the fierce and compassionate embodiment of Divine Feminine power

Maha Bandha - the "great lock" that is performed when all three major bandhas, Mula, Uddiyana, and Jalandhara, are all performed together

Mahabharata - a great Sanskrit epic narrative of over 100,000 verses that blends history, mythology, philosophy, and spiritual teachings, of which *The Bhagavad Gita* is a part

Mahima - the second siddhi, said to assist the yogi in expanding the body infinitely larger

Manipura - the third chakra, located at the solar plexus, the seat of our will, known for assisting with courage and internal fire

Manomaya Kosha - mind sheath, the kosha/layer related to thoughts and emotions of the human person

Mantras - sacred Sanskrit sounds, syllables, words, or phrases chanted, whispered, or meditated upon

Matras - Sanskrit for "measure" that can be used for measuring breath or meter of sound or other measurable items

Meditation - a deliberate practice of training the mind to achieve a state of focused awareness, calm, and heightened consciousness

Mula Bandha - the root lock created when the muscles of the pelvic floor around the perineum are contracted

Muladhara - the first chakra at the base of the spine, known for being the root or foundation

Nadi/Nadis - a channel that energy/prana follows both within and around the body

Nadi Shodhana - a type of breathing where each nostril is closed, one at a time, to increase the flow of energy through two of the main Nadi channels (Ida and Punghula)

Namaskar - ritualistic bowing, in yoga, often used to describe a series of postures as in Surya Namaskar or Sun Salutation

Namaste - a greeting, farewell, or sign of respect where one bows to another, often translated as "the divine light in me honors the divine light in you"

Nirvana - a Buddhist concept referring to a state of enlightenment, free from suffering

Niyama - the second of the eight limbs, meaning restraints or disciplines, of which there are five: Saucha, Santosha, Tapas, Svadyaya, and Ishvara Pranidhana.

Odin - the Norse god known as the "All-Father"

Om Swastyasta - a traditional Balinese greeting that means well-wishes and respect

Paramahansa Yogananda - author of Autobiography of a Yogi

Prakamya - the sixth siddhi, said to allow the yogi to materialize anywhere, anytime

Prana/Pranic - simplified as "life force energy," the fundamental energy that flows through the nadis and is behind all living things

Pranayama - breathing practices that increase pranic energy in the body

Pranamaya Kosha - vital energy sheath, the kosha/layer of vital energy tied to the breath

Prapti - the fifth siddhi, said to give the yogi unrestricted access to all places

Pratyahara - the fifth of the eight limbs, meaning sensory withdrawal, where the yogi withdraws from the external senses

Raga - the third klesha, meaning attachment

Rig Veda - a selection of 1028 Sanskrit hymns to various Hindu deities, said to be the oldest written religious text in the world

Raja - the "Royal" yoga, often used to describe the yoga style of Patanjali's eightfold path

Sahasrara - the seventh chakra, located at the crown of the head, associated with liberation and divine connection

Samadhi - the final of the eight limbs, the culmination of a yogi's years of practice, finally attaining enlightenment/bliss

Sanskrit - one of the oldest living languages said to have been realized by the sages while in heightened states of consciousness and used as the language of yoga

Santosha - the second Niyama, meaning contentment

Satya - the second Yama, meaning truthfulness

Saucha - the first Niyama, meaning cleanliness

Sawadee-ka - Traditional Thai greeting for women

Sawadee-krup - Traditional Thai greeting for men

Shakti - the feminine principle, spark of creation

Shala - Shala means house or abode. "Yoga Shala" is a dedicated space where yoga is taught and practiced that evokes a strong sense of community

Sheetali - an unusual type of breathing that is known to be cooling and assists in staving off hunger

Shiva - Hindu destroyer god, lord of Yoga, part of the trinity in Hinduism along with Brahma (the Creator) and Vishnu (the Preserver)

Siddhis - the accomplishments or supernatural powers that are said to come from a yogi's aster practice

Sivananda - style of Hatha Yoga focused on unifying body, mind, and spirit, founded by Swami Sivananda, who wrote over 300 books on yoga

Svadhisthana - the second chakra, located at the sacral plexus, known as the "joy" or "pleasure" center

Svadyaya - the fourth Niyama, referring to the study of scriptures

Tantra - Sanskrit for "weave" or "system"; this form of yoga seeks to integrate body, mind, and spirit, using a variety of tools but with a focus on the energetic components of all that is

Tapas - the third Niyama, meaning purifying practices, heat

The Yoga Sutras of Patanjali - the first codified collection of yoga knowledge written down by the sage Patanjali between 200 and 400 BCE that provides a foundation for most classical schools of yoga

Uddiyana Bandha - the abdominal lock performed when the muscles under the ribcage are contracted in and upward, believed to lift the energy upward

Ujjayi - a type of breathing often referred to as "ocean sounding" breath due to the sound created while restricting the back of the throat

Upanishad - Hindu scriptures that discuss philosophy, meditation, and the nature of God, said to be mystical contemplations on the Vedas

Vasitva - the eighth and final siddhi, said to allow the yogi to control all the material elements and natural forces

Vedas - a large group of Hindu scriptures, sacred knowledge, and holy learning, arguably the oldest surviving on earth

Vinyasa - a stylized form of Hatha yoga linking the breath to the movement of the body

Visuddha - the fifth chakra, located at the throat, known as the communication center, also responsible for detoxification

Vjnanamaya Kosha - wisdom body, the kosha/layer of the human person associated with intellect and intuition

Wakan Tanka - translated as "Great Spirit" or "Great Mystery" to the Lakota Native Americans

Yahweh - the most sacred name in Judaism, referring to God

Yama - the first of the eight limbs

Yin - from Chinese, particularly Taoist, philosophy, it is the feminine, receiving principle of the universe, complementing the "yang" masculine, active principle

Yoga - See Chapter 5 because I did a pretty good job describing it already, or did you skip right to the glossary?

Yoga Nidra - this yogic sleep is a guided relaxation technique found to be a deeply restorative practice that lies between the area of meditation and sleep

Yogi - a practitioner of yoga, sometimes used to describe the masculine principle, but commonly used for all those who practice

Yogini - a feminine practitioner of yoga, in Tantric traditions, is linked to Shakti/goddess worship

OTHER BOOKS BY TRACEY

The Accidental Yogini Series:
The Accidental Yogini: Kristin
The Accidental Yogini: Padma
The Accidental Yogini: Ruth (due 2025)
(and more coming)

The Tia Brooks Trilogy:
Butterfly
Wolf
Raven

Co-Author Books:
Love Initiation: Learning the Language of Soul
Stories from the Yogic Heart
Yoga in America

Tracey's Amazon Author Page:
https://www.amazon.com/stores/Tracey-L.-Ulshafer/author/

www.TraceyUlshafer.com
www.OneYogaCenter.net

"THE VAULT" YOGA

"The Vault" holds treasured curated yoga classes taught by Rev. Dr. Tracey. You can practice her many themed yoga classes for all levels with a small monthly subscription. With a simple internet connection, you can practice yoga anywhere, anytime. Inside The Vault, you'll find these types of classes with modifications and variations for all levels:
- Chair Yoga
- Gentle Yoga
- Hatha Yoga
- Vinyasa Yoga
- Restorative Yoga
- Yin Yoga
- Meditation
- Short Practices

Other Specialty Playlists on The Vault:
- Wheel of the Year
- Animal Energy Medicine
- Stretch Classes
- Divine Feminine - The Goddess
- Chakra Yoga Classes
- Sun/Moon/Stars
- 12-Step Recovery Chair Yoga

Subscribe to The Vault today:
https://www.oneyogacenter.net/yoga-classes

ABOUT THE AUTHOR

Rev. Dr. Tracey L. Ulshafer is the founder of One Yoga and Wellness Center, which operated as a physical studio in New Jersey until 2022. Dr. Tracey continues to escort international yoga and healing retreats. Her self-published, award-winning fictional book, *The Accidental Yogini*, continues to be praised as an easy read with digestible yoga philosophies spread throughout. The book was rebranded as a series in 2024 as *The Accidental Yogini: Kristin,* and a new book, *The Accidental Yogini: Padma,* was also released, with more books to come. Tracey now continues to offer her unique brand of Hatha Yoga and classes on Thai Yoga Bodywork and other yogic principles both virtually and as pop-up workshops. With a Doctorate in Ministries, she has studied world religions, and as an Interfaith minister, she designs ceremonies and rituals that ring of Timeless Trueness. Since closing the studio, Tracey has devoted more time to her passions of writing and producing her documentary series, *The Earth Chakras*.

www.ingramcontent.com/pod-product-compliance
Lightning Source LLC
Chambersburg PA
CBHW022144160426
43197CB00009B/1420